The Blessed Hope of the Church

Book #2 of the Son of Man Series

J.L. Reintgen

WestBow
PRESS
A DIVISION OF THOMAS NELSON

WestBow Press books may be ordered through booksellers or by contacting:

WestBow Press
A Division of Thomas Nelson
1663 Liberty Drive
Bloomington, IN 47403
www.westbowpress.com
1-(866) 928-1240

ISBN: 978-1-4497-9763-8 (sc)
ISBN: 978-1-4497-9764-5 (hc)
ISBN: 978-1-4497-9483-5 (e)

Library of Congress Control Number: 2013910619

Printed in the United States of America.

WestBow Press rev. date: 06/12/2014

Contents

Preface

The Spirit of God through Paul tells us those who are in the flesh cannot please God (Rom. 8:8). If we are spiritually wise we will realize that this is not describing the behavior of a man from moment to moment, or day to day. Rather, it is identifying one of two possible spiritual positions that any man can be found in. The following verse verifies this statement as the truth by identifying the second and alternate position – that of being 'in the Spirit.' (Rom. 8:9)

"But you are not in the flesh but in the Spirit, if indeed the Spirit of God dwells in you. Now if anyone does not have the Spirit of Christ, he is not His."

'In the Spirit' is the true Christian position. It is having been sealed by the Spirit, by which in fact, the Spirit of God dwells in you, the Spirit of adoption by whom we cry, "Abba, Father." (Rom. 8:15). True believers have been sealed by God's seal of authenticity, and He knows, in divine simplicity, those who are His (II Tim. 2:19). All true believers are 'in the Spirit' *because* the Spirit of God dwells in them. This is the believer's position before God.

Paul does say, 'if indeed.' It is not overtly obvious to Paul or any man as to who has been sealed by the Spirit. We may see evidence of this position in some people if we can follow them around long enough. The simple truth is that man cannot see this seal. It is obvious to God and all in the unseen spirit realm – angels and demons – but not something obvious to man. The fact remains, if you do not have the Spirit of Christ, you are not a believer, you are not a true Christian (I John 4:13).

Those who do not possess the Spirit have a position of 'in the flesh.' This position is one and the same as being 'in Adam,' the first man. This position is the state of all men by physical birth. The only exception to this reality was the virgin birth of Jesus. Through the redemptive work of Jesus Christ, the believer is now 'in the Spirit,' or also known as 'in Christ,' the second Adam. This is the position of all true believers.

The Christian has a heavenly calling (Heb. 3:1). The believer has a citizenship in heaven (Phil. 3:20). We presently have been made to sit in heavenly places in Christ (Eph. 2:6). We have been blessed already with every spiritual blessing in these heavenly places in Christ (Eph. 1:3). Can the believer have any doubt that we will be physically brought into the heavens one day as the body of Christ? What would be the point of our citizenship being in heaven, if our habitation is on the earth?

The Son of Man is risen and is in the glory of His Father. He has entered the glory already. Yet it is clear, from the Scriptures, He went ahead of the believer as the forerunner for us (Heb. 6:19-20). If He is the forerunner, it is because the believer will follow Him there, behind the veil, into the very presence and glory of God. The believer's hope is both sure and steadfast, and presently this hope enters in behind the veil with the forerunner. This is because we will physically enter there as well. All these truths are due to the believer's true position 'in Christ' and the privilege that this position affords.

This book should be a blessing for all believers to read. It is the use of Scripture in proving the absolute validity of the doctrine of the rapture of the church as part of the counsels and plan of God. For the professing church world this book should be a last minute re-awakening. In one sense it is part of a midnight cry that has already been sounded (Matt. 25:6). Yet I fear it is a cry which has already been taken for granted and discarded by many. But we do what we can by the grace God has given us.

For the believer there are three views of Christ of great significance, to which all our thoughts and doctrines must answer. First, there is Christ on the cross. This is the foundational work of all God's counsels and it is the purchased redemption of all believers, His blood and His death being the price and propitiation for all grace given to us. The second is Christ sitting at the right hand of God. This is the reason the Holy Spirit was sent down, and that the Holy Spirit gathers a body. The church doesn't exist until the Head of the body was exalted in glory (Eph. 1:20-23). The doctrine of the church – what it is, how it was formed, what its calling is, where it is going – is not revealed until Paul is called and fashioned by the sovereign working of God. The third view is Christ coming for the church. This is the Church's true hope. Jesus will come and receive all the saints to Himself. From that point on we will experience unhindered access to both the Father and the Son. We will be in the Presence (Heb. 6:19). We will be in the glory (Rom. 3:23, Col. 1:27).

ON A PERSONAL NOTE: This book, 'The Blessed Hope of the Church,' was written differently than the first book in the series, 'The Son of Man Glorified.' In the first book I chased many rabbits around in the text of the chapters. However in this book, in each chapter, I use 'endnotes' to present related thoughts and teaching that do not properly fit in the flow of the text. These references are numbered in the text and the endnotes are found at the end of each chapter.

The first book was a broad based work on biblical theology. It was designed to show the biblical principles needed to understand the counsels of God. As a believer, if you know the plan of God and the biblical principles that order that plan, what more do you need? This plan will not change. And Jesus said, "No longer do I call you servants, for the servant does not know what the master is doing." (John 15:15).

Some may say it is more important that we know God rather than know His counsels and principles. But this would be a misconception. It is by what God has said and all that He has done that He is revealed to us. Only by the work of the cross do we know and see the love of God for us (Rom. 5:5-11). By this same work we understand that God is a holy and righteous God without measure, condemning His own Son for us (Rom. 3:23-26). When we see what Jehovah does for a Jewish remnant in the end, we know that our God is faithful, beyond any doubt, to fulfill all that He has promised. Through the revelation of God's counsels for the church, existing before the foundations of the world, we see and know the one true living God as the Sovereign.

1 Corinthians 2:9-10

"But as it is written:
"Eye has not seen, nor ear heard,
Nor have entered into the heart of man
The things which God has prepared for those who love Him."

(10) But God has revealed them to us through His Spirit. For the Spirit searches all things, yes, the deep things of God."

The true believer has been sealed by His Spirit. We have been given the Spirit of truth and have the 'mind of Christ.' God has done so for us through our redemption in Christ so that we would be His friends and confidantes. He wants the believer to know His thoughts, His mind, His counsels and purposes. When we read the entire passage from which the above comes (I Cor. 1:17-2:16), it becomes evident the Spirit isn't referring to theological seminaries, dependence on clergy, or a mastery of the Hebrew and Greek languages. These things may serve some place, and often are highly regarded in the eyes of men, but the Spirit doesn't give them mention in the passage. The truth is simple – for the believer it is the given Spirit of God that teaches the mind and thoughts of God, and reveals all the things God has prepared for us.

This book is about one of those things of God that 'eye has not seen, ear has not heard, and it hasn't entered into the heart of natural man.' This thing of God's can only be known by the church through His Word taught by the Holy Spirit. This second book is written to prove from the Scriptures a specific doctrine – the rapture, the blessed hope of the church. Again, you will need your Bible by your side, for there are many quoted and referenced Scriptures. Hopefully your Bible is a sound and reliable translation. In this book I use, almost exclusively, the New King James translation for quotes.

God bless you in your studies. May the Spirit of God use this book to show you many valuable understandings. Always seek the thoughts of God rather than the teachings of men. The failure to do so has been the ruin of the church world. Always pursue sound doctrine, which can only come from the Word of God taught by His Holy Spirit. Jesus is coming soon. His last words spoken to the church are these, "Surely I am coming quickly."

The true church then responds, "Amen. Even so, come, Lord Jesus!"

Chapter 1:

The Promise of Christ

efore Jesus was arrested and put on trial to be crucified, He spent the good part of the evening with His disciples. He was sharing and teaching many things. The disciples would not understand at that time all the things He was sharing, but they eventually would see things more clearly when the promised Spirit was given to them. These were not just simple instructions, but much of what He shared were promises and words of comfort. This One they had walked with and spent their time with for the last three and a half years was about to depart from them. He had met all their needs and protected and kept them all this time, bearing with their weaknesses and infirmities. While He was on the earth He perfectly kept all those given to Him by the Father (John 17:6-13).

The emotional state of the disciples had to be intense. Sorrow, fear, and confusion had to be a part of what they were experiencing. They had to be feeling isolated and forsaken as well. Into this setting and at this critical moment, the Lord Jesus, ever so gracious and always aware of the full importance of His circumstances and surroundings, speaks these comforting words to the disciples in the form of a promise.

John 14:1-4

"Let not your heart be troubled; you believe in God, believe also in Me. In My Father's house are many mansions; if it were not so, I would have told you. I go to prepare a place for you. And if I go and prepare a place for you, I will come again and receive you to Myself; that where I am, there you may be also. And where I go you know, and the way you know."

This is a promise for all true believers, not just the eleven that were with Him. We can reason it is for all believers because the greater part of the promise remains unfulfilled. He has not yet come again and received anyone to Himself with the intention that where He went He would take them also. But this promise from Jesus was divine comfort to the disciples at that time. Comfort and peace as given by Him to His own. Not in the character and nature as the world gives comfort.

John 14:27-28

"Peace I leave with you, My peace I give to you; not as the world gives do I give to you. Let not your heart be troubled, neither let it be afraid. You have heard Me say to you, 'I am going away and coming back to you.' If you loved Me, you would rejoice because I said, 'I am going to the Father,' for My Father is greater than I."

His Promise is Comfort, Peace, and Joy now

This is very similar to what He said earlier in the same chapter, and He calls this to their attention – that He is going away, but He would return back to them. His peace given to the believer, in the midst of fears and apprehensions upon His departure from them out of this world or from His absence from us now, is based on the promise that He would come back for us.

The Lord gives comfort and peace to the believer that cannot be found or acquired from this world. *"In the world you will have* tribulation," (John 16:33). This is what the true believer receives from the world. Also the believer is hated by the world, because He stands apart from the world as Christ does (John 15:18-19). We have been left in this world, but not as part of it. It is not just that the Lord departed from us that gave rise to our discomfort, but that we have been left in a world that we are no longer a part of.

John 17:13-16

"But now I come to You, and these things I speak in the world, that they may have My joy fulfilled in themselves. I have given them Your word; and the world has hated them because they are not of the world, just as I am not of the world. I do not pray that You should take them out of the world, but that You should keep them from the evil one. They are not of the world, just as I am not of the world."

He also gives us His joy to be ours while He is away. This divine joy is ours based on the same understanding we are to have concerning the world – believers are set apart from the world and this world doesn't have divine joy to give. The understanding of the Lord's words is in the truth that He is separated from the world, having now ended any relationship with it. And if He is not of the world then we are not of the world. If the believer had a relationship with the world it would be one that is inappropriate. The declaration of Christ's complete separation from this world is uniquely spoken by Him earlier in John's gospel.

God condemns the World; Jesus is lifted up apart from it

John 12:31-32

"Now is the judgment of this world; now the ruler of this world will be cast out. And I, if I am lifted up from the earth, will draw all peoples to Myself."

At this time God had fully condemned the entire world. The lifting up of the Son of Man would be the end of any relationship Christ had with the world He had created and into which He was sent by the Father (John 1:10). The world did not know Him. He came to His own, but the Jews did not receive Him. They rejected Him and put Him to death. God had fully tested the responsibility of man, who by nature was descended from Adam, and found absolutely no fruit whatsoever (Matt. 21:19). Man was proven lost, without resources, and a child destined for wrath (Eph. 2:2-3). The sending of the Jewish Messiah to Israel was the final testing by God. They were God's most privileged people. When they failed this last testing, by it God condemned the whole world (Rom. 3:19).[1]

The Believer is lifted up apart from the World

Jesus Christ, as the Son of Man, is lifted up apart from the earth and world. He has no relationship at all with the world that is judged.[2] Those He draws to Himself are believers, as chosen by God from out of the condemned world (John 15:19, 17:6). They are associated with Him as lifted up apart from the earth and world. These are of the heavenly calling in Christ Jesus, and not of the earth (Heb. 3:1). And they are the ones He prays for that last evening He spent with them.

John 17:9-10

"I pray for them. I do not pray for the world but for those whom You have given Me, for they are Yours. And all Mine are Yours, and Yours are Mine, and I am glorified in them."

John 17:20

"I do not pray for these alone, but also for those who will believe in Me through their word."

He does not pray for the condemned world, but rather for those given to Him out of the world by the Father. He prayed for all believers, those who would be drawn to Him by God through the testimony of these eyewitnesses (John 15:27). But all these passages, particularly those from John's gospel, serve to develop the full meaning of Christ's and the believer's separation from this present evil world. This understanding then brings us to these words He spoke that evening.

Jesus is Departing the World; He cannot stay here

John 17:11-16

(11) "Now I am no longer in the world, but these are in the world, and I come to You. Holy Father, keep through Your name those whom You have given Me, that they may be one as We are. (12) While I was with them in the world, I kept them in Your name. Those whom You gave Me I have kept, and none of them is lost except the son of perdition, that the Scripture might be fulfilled. (13) But now I come to You, and these things I speak in the world, that they may have My joy fulfilled in themselves. (14) I have given them Your word; and the world has hated them because they are not of the world, just as I am not of the world. (15) I do not pray that You should take them out of the world, but that You should keep them from the evil one. (16) They are not of the world, just as I am not of the world.

He certainly was departing this world and going to the Father. He would be leaving them behind. There are simply many spiritual truths associated with His leaving. As the Son of Man He would be the forerunner for all believers into the presence and glory of God. He would be the firstborn from among the dead and the firstborn among many brethren. As the perfect and eternal sacrifice it would be necessary that His blood be brought into the tabernacle in the heavens made without hands (Heb. 9:11), into the presence of God for us (Heb. 9:23-26). In this one time work He is both the better sacrifice and the better High Priest carrying in the blood of propitiation. This Man, after He had offered one sacrifice for sins, sat down in perpetuity at the right hand of God (Heb. 10:12). The sitting down is only indicative of an eternally accepted sacrifice highly pleasing and satisfying to God – a work perfectly and completely finished (Heb. 10:1-14). Until Jesus was glorified in this manner, the Holy Spirit could not be sent down, the seal of God in the believer by which our bodies are the temple of God (John 7:39, 16:17).

All these are blessed truths associated with His having to depart this world. But we sense something entirely different in the above quoted passage. Somehow the world itself is prohibiting His continued presence in it. He speaks of leaving, or even as already having left the world when He prays, *"Now I am no longer in the world...and I come to You, Holy Father..."* Yet the disciples would be left behind for He says, *"...but these are in the world...I do not pray that You should take them out of the world..."* What is so prominent in our Lord's words and the character of John's Holy Spirit inspired gospel is the thought and teaching of absolute separation from this present condemned world. It is a setting apart of both the Son of Man lifted up (John 12:32) and all believers united to Him (John 14:19-20). Therefore He also remarks, *"...and the world has hated them because they are not of the world, just as I am not of the world."*

The World is condemned; it is only Defilement.

The believer's position in relation to the world is the same as His – a relationship with the world doesn't exist any longer.[3] The world is condemned, He is lifted up apart from it all, and we are associated and united with Him, so much so, He is in us and we are in Him. But He is departing out of this world and He tells us we have to stay behind. Why?

There was a difference between the Lord and believers at this time that is the basis and reason for His departure and their having to remain behind. As the Son of Man lifted up apart from the world He would have a resurrected glorified body (John 20:27). This world, condemned in its own sin (John 8:21, 9:39-41, 12:31, 15:22-24), would only be defilement for Him if He stayed here in the resurrected state (John 20:17). He came into the world He had created looking for fruit, but found none. This world is guilty of rejecting Him. He no longer has any relationship with it because the relationship itself would be defilement to the Son of Man lifted up. He cannot stay down here in this defiled place, so He is going away to prepare a place for us.

Being present in this evil world is defilement for anything that is 'of God.' This is easily seen as the case for Jesus in the time after His resurrection and before His final ascension. He never appears to the world, to those of the unbelieving world. He only appears to His own, those He was given by the Father out of the world (John 17:1-6). All of them would become eye-witnesses in testimony of His resurrection (I Cor. 15:4-7). These are the ones that were already pure by the word He had spoken to them (John 15:3, 17:17) and so there would be no defilement in appearing to them.

John 12:23-32

(23) "'But Jesus answered them, saying, "The hour has come that the Son of Man should be glorified. (24) Most assuredly, I say to you, unless a grain of wheat falls into the ground and dies, it remains alone; but if it dies, it produces much grain. (25) He who loves his life will lose it, and he who hates his life in this world will keep it for eternal life. (26) If anyone serves Me, let him follow Me; and where I am, there My servant will be also. If anyone serves Me, him My Father will honor.

(27) "Now My soul is troubled, and what shall I say? 'Father, save Me from this hour'? But for this purpose I came to this hour. (28) Father, glorify Your name."

Then a voice came from heaven, saying, "I have both glorified it and will glorify it again."

(29) Therefore the people who stood by and heard it said that it had thundered. Others said, "An angel has spoken to Him."

(30) Jesus answered and said, "This voice did not come because of Me, but for your sake. (31) Now is the judgment of this world; now the ruler of this world will be cast out. (32) And I, if I am lifted up from the earth, will draw all peoples to Myself."

The Glory of God manifested in the Glorified Son of Man

I want to step back from the minute detail of this passage and consider its context and the general truths presented in it. Jesus is the Son of Man who would be glorified. It would be God who would glorify Him after the Son of Man accomplished a certain work which first perfectly glorified God (please read John 13:31-32). This work is the foundation by which all God's counsels are to be accomplished. This work is the Son of Man as the single grain of wheat that must fall to the ground and die. By His death the righteousness and holiness of God was maintained, satisfied, and fully glorified.

God therefore glorified the Son of Man. All the counsels of God, all His workings, result in His own glory. This is accomplished by all the glory of God centering on Jesus Christ, the now glorified Son of Man – all things in heaven and all things on earth – in Him (Eph. 1:10). If the Son of Man glorified God, then God would glorify Him immediately. God begins this by raising Christ from the dead and exalting Him far above everything to the right hand of God (Eph. 1:19-23). There He now sits, as the Son of Man, crowned with glory and honor (Heb. 2:9).

There is also the glory from eternity past that the Father shared with the Son (John 17:5). The Father would again share His glory with Him upon His return, for Jesus prays, *"And now, O Father, glorify Me together with Yourself..."* However, we must understand this distinction. Christ re-enters God's glory as the Son of Man raised up and exalted. He re-enters the glory as a Man. In the above quoted passage from John 12, the glory of God is in view, and He would be glorified in all that was about to take place. He would be glorified in the grain of wheat dying, in the Son of Man being set apart from the earth, and in His holy and righteous judgment of the world.

Life in the First Adam

The contrast of Christ and the believer to the world is brought out even more so in verse 25 of the above quoted passage. He who loves his present life in this world will lose it. This is life in the first Adam and part of this world. This life is to be hated and put to death, ending your relationship with Adam and the world. Life in the first Adam must be crucified with Christ (Rom. 6:6, Gal. 2:20). It is only through death you can end your relationship with this present evil world (Gal. 6:14). It is only through death – through following Him – that the individual will be found where He is. And where is He? He is certainly apart from the world. Where did He go? He went into the glory of God (v.26).

It is important to have a clear understanding of the distinction made by the Holy Spirit in this gospel between the believer and the world. By it we better understand the promise the Lord spoke to them as comfort. Let us look at the promise now more closely.

John 14:1-4

(1) "Let not your heart be troubled; you believe in God, believe also in Me. (2) In My Father's house are many mansions; if it were not so, I would have told you. I go to prepare a place for you. (3) And if I go and prepare a place for you, I will come again and receive you to Myself; that where I am, there you may be also. (4) And where I go you know, and the way you know."

The Lord's words and promise bring up two questions from Thomas, which He patiently answers in turn.

- How can we know the way? Jesus' answer is that He is the way and it is through Him. The believer is 'in Christ' and united to Him.

- Lord, where are You going? His answer is that He is going to the Father.

It should be easily understood that He was departing this world and going to His Father. The Father was not somewhere in Jerusalem, Judea, Samaria, or Galilee. He wasn't anywhere on this earth and in this world. The Lord's promise to all believers boils down to this – He will personally come from where He went and where He presently is, and take us to the Father. He will come from the Father and take us back to the Father.

The Glorified Body

It is obvious Christ is departing this world. It is also obvious the disciples would remain in this world, being comforted with the sure hope of our Lord's promise. As for the disciples left behind, the glorified body is the difference between themselves and the Lord. The Son of Man would be raised and in a glorified body, and for Him to remain in this world would only be defilement. The believer would not have a glorified body like Jesus, at least not yet.

John 13:33

"Little children, I shall be with you a little while longer. You will seek Me; and as I said to the Jews, 'Where I am going, you cannot come,' so now I say to you."

John 13:36

"Simon Peter said to Him, "Lord, where are You going?"

Jesus answered him, "Where I am going you cannot follow Me now, but you shall follow Me afterward."

Jesus is leaving the world, while the disciples would have to remain behind. He is going away. They cannot follow Him now, but they would certainly follow Him later. This is the difference between what He promises all those who are His own and what He speaks to the condemned world. Those who are His are associated with Him – they are not of the world as He is not of the world. When the Holy Spirit was sent down to them (for this is the understanding of all the similar phrases in the Lord's discourse here that start with the words, *"In that day..."* John 15:20), they would eventually comprehend their union to Him – you in Me, and I in you. But sin would remain in their bodies of flesh and they would not be able to go where Christ was going *at that time*.

The World cannot follow Christ to where He went

It is never the thought that believers cannot go where He is, but rather they cannot go yet (John 13:36). However, the world and all those of the world simply cannot go period! This is an impossibility confirmed by the Lord's words spoken to the Jews previously in this gospel.

John 7:33-34

"Then Jesus said to them, "I shall be with you a little while longer, and then I go to Him who sent Me. You will seek Me and not find Me, and where I am you cannot come."

John 8:21

"Then Jesus said to them again, "I am going away, and you will seek Me, and will die in your sin. Where I go you cannot come."

Here Jesus distinguishes between His followers and the world. What He said to the Jews are His words to the unbelieving world which is condemned. The world, including the Jewish people, is not associated with Him. They will die in their sins – the whole world will die in their sins. This is the judgment that stands over the entire world and those who are part of the world. As we've said previously, when the Son of Man was lifted up from the earth (John 12:32) it meant the end of any relationship He had with the world. And now He is speaking of His physical departure out of this world. His separation is morally, spiritually, but also physically from this world. It is simply impossible for those of the world to follow Him.

John 8:23-24

"And He said to them, "You are from beneath; I am from above. You are of this world; I am not of this world. Therefore I said to you that you will die in your sins; for if you do not believe that I am He, you will die in your sins."

The overall emphasis of the separation from the world continues throughout this gospel. It is one of the major themes of the Spirit through John. *"You are of this world; I am not..."* And again the condemnation of what is 'from beneath' is repeated. As the Son of Man He has been given all judgment (John 5:22, 27) and He certainly implies He has judged the world (John 8:26).

The Believer follows Christ to where He has gone

Yet He never speaks this way to the disciples. He never implies any of these things concerning believers. They are not of the world as He is not of the world. He promises them that He will personally take them to be where He has gone. It then becomes clear that it would have to be in the same manner in which He went – in a resurrected glorified body.

As believers we will need the sin nature removed from our flesh and our bodies glorified. This will be necessary in order to enter into the presence of the Father. And once our bodies are glorified as our Lord's, this world will no longer be a fit place for us to remain in. This physical change is what Paul speaks of to the Corinthians.

2 Corinthians 5:4

"For we who are in this tent groan, being burdened, not because we want to be unclothed, but further clothed, that mortality may be swallowed up by life."

In order for the believer to follow Christ where He has gone he needs for his mortality to be 'swallowed up by life.' Specifically this refers to those who are in Christ and still alive on this earth when God demonstrates His exceedingly great power towards us at the time of this event. They are the ones specifically spoken of in the scriptures as mortality putting on immortality (I Cor. 15:53-54). They are those referred to by the apostle when he says, *"We shall not all sleep..."* (I Cor. 15:51), and again when he says, *"... we who are alive and remain..."* (I Thess. 4:15, 17) In the verse above it is *"...we who are in this tent groan, being burdened..."* It is all those in Christ who are still in this present physical body on the earth.

However, many believers have also fallen asleep in Christ. Death will not exclude them from this event. They are the ones specifically referred to in the scriptures as corruption putting on incorruption (I Cor. 15:50-54). These are the ones the apostle speaks of in saying, *"...I do not want you to be ignorant, brethren, concerning those who have fallen asleep...those who sleep in Jesus...will by no means precede those who are asleep...the dead in Christ will rise first."* (I Thess. 4:13-16) Again the apostle speaks of *"...those who have fallen asleep in Christ..."* (I Cor. 15:18)

Not to be Unclothed, but further Clothed

In the above quoted verse from II Corinthians 5, the state of those asleep in Christ is described as being 'unclothed' or naked. This state is being absent from the body while it is corrupting in the grave. It is the believer's spirit and soul present with the Lord, which is described as far better than being still in this tent groaning and burdened. The death of a believer is not to be feared, for it is truly a state of greater blessing than life on this earth. If our thoughts and feelings about these two distinct states were known, it would reveal much about what is in our hearts as believers. To be absent from the body is to be present with the Lord – it is the thought of being with Jesus that creates all the believer's proper desires and affections.[4] But this is veering off the particular direction of this chapter, so I'll attempt to better address these thoughts later in the book. This teaching establishes the reality of three different and distinct states for the believer.

1) ***Being present in the body on the earth is to be absent from the Lord.*** At the first this was the state of all the disciples. The Lord had departed from this world and they were left behind. It is the state in which we groan within ourselves, being burdened (Rom. 8:23, II Cor. 5:4). But in this state the Lord did not leave us comfortless, but gave all believers another Comforter, the Spirit of truth who abides with us now forever. This same Spirit, while the believer is still present in the body, constantly makes intercession for us with groanings which cannot be uttered, and this always according to the perfect will of God (Rom. 8:26-27). Also the Lord left His promise that He would personally return for all believers, by which the indwelling Spirit becomes God's guarantee that such promise is our sure and steadfast hope (Rom. 8:23-25).

13

2) ***Being absent from the body is to be present with the Lord.*** However this is the state of being unclothed and naked (II Cor. 5:3-4), where spirit and soul departs to be with the Lord, and the body is corrupting in the grave. This is a far better state than the previous one, yet it is not one that the believer is to properly desire. The apostle says, "...not because we want to be unclothed..." It is not what we want, nor is it the blessed hope of the believer. It is scripturally described as being asleep in Christ. But death is not what the Lord promised the believer. Death is not the reason He returns for us.

3) ***The final state of the true believer is not to be unclothed, but further clothed, that mortality may be swallowed up by life*** (II Cor. 5:4, Rom. 8:11). For all those who are asleep in Christ it is resurrection from among the dead. It is the corrupted state putting on incorruption. For both, the alive and asleep in Christ, it is what the apostle says, *"...we shall all be changed – in a moment, in the twinkling of an eye...the dead will be raised incorruptible, and we shall be changed."* (I Cor. 15:51-54). It is the time when sin is removed from the flesh, the adoption, the redemption of the body (Rom. 8:23). It is the glorified body, the glorified state, by which we will be enabled to enter the very presence and glory of the Father God.

Jesus' Promise is not about Death

Some will say that the Lord's promise at the beginning of John 14 is referring to the death of the believer. That simply is false teaching and gross misunderstanding, especially when you consider what the Holy Spirit is emphasizing in John's gospel and our Lord's words – it is Christ's and the believer's complete separation from this condemned world. Jesus is departing the world, but promises to return, at God's appropriate time, and take all believers into the presence of the Father. If this was the death of the believer, it would mean that the Lord was promising to come thousands upon thousands of times. If it was referencing death, then it is the unclothed condition with the body left behind for corruption. Without the body the individual is not a complete man. Death is not the promise here, but rather it is *resurrection and life.*

For the disciples it was obvious that Jesus departing from them was distressing; to be with Him was comforting. He had to leave the world. But He knew what to speak to them, for He gives them the promise of His own word. He tells them, *"I will come again and receive you to Myself; that where I am, there you may be also."* God's own Word is the basis of all our comfort and certainty. This is the blessed hope of the believer. This is the blessed hope of the church.

Chapter 1: Endnotes

[1] The understanding of the principle of responsibility in man and how God fully tested it is thoroughly discussed in the first book in this series, 'The Son of Man Glorified.' When God tests man in this principle it is symbolically represented in Scripture as God looking for fruit. Man is proven as always failing in responsibility and this is the story of man and of Scripture. Man's responsibility is his works. When any man is judged by God on his own works, it is certain condemnation and wrath. God's testing of responsibility in man came to an end when Messiah was presented to Israel. The parable in Matt. 21:33-40 depicts God's testing of Israel when they represented all mankind in the first Adam. The cursing of the fig tree in Matt. 21:19 represents the outcome and final test results for man, again represented by Israel as the most privileged nation on earth. At that time God condemns the entire world (John 12:31, Rom. 3:19).

[2] The lifting up of the Son of Man in John 12 has a different emphasis of meaning than that found in John 3:14, although the phrasing is similar. In John 3 it is the use of a teaching instrument called types or shadows – the lifting up of Christ on the cross is prefigured by Moses lifting up the serpent in the wilderness on a pole. The symbols found in all types are used for their similarities and contrasts to teach spiritual truths and realities. All types/shadows precede their fulfillments/substance. And the fulfillments and substance is always the greater value and reality. When Moses lifted up the serpent, it was judged, cursed, and condemned by Jehovah on behalf of the nation of Israel. In John 3 the Son of Man is lifted up as judged, cursed, and condemned by God on behalf of the sin of the world. In John 12 His being lifted up is His separation from the world – morally, spiritually, and ultimately physically in His glorification.

[3] The Son of Man lifted up is a reference to His death on the cross. By His death He has ended any relationship with the world. The principle is 'until death do you part' with death ending the relationship. Jesus goes on to identify the believer as not of the world just as He is not of the world (John 17:14). In the epistles this redemptive truth is explained in greater detail – it is by our death we are separated from the world. It is because we have died with Christ (Col. 2:20, Gal. 6:14).

[4] Whenever death is actually spoken of in the epistles it is always with this understanding – to be absent from the body is to be present with the Lord (II Cor. 5:8). The true believer's proper desires and affections are in Christ

and with Christ. If the Lord tarries, most of us as believers will sleep in Christ. The earthly body corrupts in the grave, but spirit and soul depart and go to be with the Lord. This is described scripturally as being unclothed or naked, yet also always described as a well pleasing or far better state (II Cor. 5:8, Phil. 1:21,23). Why? – Because we are in the presence of our Lord. Now it is never described as 'going to heaven' although this is true, but that thought is not where our proper affections should be. Also it is not properly a 'going on to glory' because the believer's entrance into God's glory will not be until he has the glorified body. One last distinction concerning death – it is the believer leaving his earthly body behind and going on to be with the Lord in heaven. It is never described in scripture as 'the Lord coming' or 'the Lord coming back' for us.

Notes

Chapter 2:

The Details of the Rapture

The word 'rapture' isn't found in the Scriptures. Rather, it is a word that is commonly used in naming a certain event that is found in the Scriptures. This is done for convenience so that we do not have to recite large passages for others to know what we are talking about. In this sense the word is 'made up' by man, but it doesn't mean the event itself is 'made up' by man. The naysayers will tell you this is a fictitious doctrine created through the over exuberance of the human mind. But a detailed description of this event is easily found in scripture by any believer.

1 Thessalonians 4:13-18

"But I do not want you to be ignorant, brethren, concerning those who have fallen asleep, lest you sorrow as others who have no hope. For if we believe that Jesus died and rose again, even so God will bring with Him those who sleep in Jesus.

For this we say to you by the word of the Lord, that we who are alive and remain until the coming of the Lord will by no means precede those who are asleep. For the Lord Himself will descend from heaven with a shout, with the voice of an archangel, and with the trumpet of God. And the dead in Christ will rise first. Then we who are alive and remain shall be caught up together with them in the clouds to meet the Lord in the air. And thus we shall always be with the Lord. Therefore comfort one another with these words."

The Rapture includes the entire Body of Christ

It would be my hope that every true believer would be very hesitant to deny that this event will happen at some future point in time exactly as these words describe. Otherwise, if we do not believe these words we should throw our bibles away. But what is done in unbelief in many cases and teaching is to add some additional thoughts at the end of verse 17 above. We meet the Lord in the air but what is added is a U-turn performed in the clouds and a return of everyone back to the earth. This ultimately is to keep everything earthly and on earth, and denies the existence of the heavenly calling of the church. This simply violates so many principles found in the Word of God concerning His counsels and ways that I hardly know where to begin in rebuttal.

The details of this passage show that this event exclusively includes the entire body of Christ, the entire church (Eph. 1:22-23). The physical bodies of all those who sleep in Christ remain in the grave. Those in Christ who are alive and remain so, are identified in the passage as on the earth as well. The physical body of the believer is his final connection to this earth, regardless of whether he is asleep or alive in Christ. This body remains on the earth through the entire time appointed by God for the church on the earth – from Pentecost and its inception to the rapture and its departing. This connection is not simply with the earth but also with the first Adam. Sin in the flesh is what Adam has given to the entire human race (Rom. 5:12, 7:25, and 8:3). When sin is removed from the believer's flesh, our final connection with Adam is severed, and our bodies will be glorified.

This World is defilement for the Glorified Body

The believer's body, having been glorified in this event, will not be suitable to stay and remain living on the earth in this world. We saw the Lord make this implication concerning Himself in His words to the disciples before His departure from them (John 17:4-17). Being a glorified Man, this world would be defilement for Jesus after His resurrection. In the exact same way and with the same spiritual reasoning, when the church is resurrected and glorified, it will be removed from this world as well.

There is no U-turn. The above passage compares quite favorably with the promise the Lord made to the disciples. In John 14 Jesus tells them, *"...I will come again and receive you to Myself, that where I am, there you may be also."* He promises to come personally, He receives them to Himself personally, and He definitively takes them from the earth to where He was previously. This is into the Father's presence in heaven – that is where He was and that is where He is presently. In the passage that follows, the Spirit says, *"For the Lord Himself will descend from heaven..."* This is the Lord personally returning for His Bride.

1 Thessalonians 4:16-17

"For the Lord Himself will descend from heaven with a shout, with the voice of an archangel, and with the trumpet of God. And the dead in Christ will rise first. Then we who are alive and remain shall be caught up together with them in the clouds to meet the Lord in the air. And thus we shall always be with the Lord."

There is no U-turn to be added. When we are caught up together into the clouds it is to be personally with Jesus in the glorified state, and to continue to go on into the presence of His Father and our Father, His God and our God (John 20:17).[5]

The Second Adam is a Life-Giving Spirit

There is another chapter in the epistles that also gives great detail concerning the rapture of the church. It is in I Corinthians 15 where we find teaching about Jesus Christ as the last Adam, the second Man (vs. 45-47). The first man Adam became a living being, but in him all die since by man came sin and death (vs. 21-22). The last Adam became a life-giving spirit. This life-giving power we experience in two distinct ways in our salvation.

- We receive eternal life by the quickening power of the Son of God (John 5:21, 26, 17:1-3) while still on the earth. Life is from the Son, as the Son of Man and through His death (John 6:53). This is a sovereign work of the Father or the Son (John 5:21, 26).

- The life-giving power of the second Adam will be demonstrated in the future event known as the 'rapture' when this life the believer possesses swallows up mortality in the glorified body (II Cor. 5:1-4). This will be the sovereign work of God, another demonstration of the sovereign grace and the exceeding greatness of His power toward us who believe (Eph. 1:18-20).

I Corinthians 15 describes the gospel of the Son of Man glorified that Paul preached (vs. 1-8). However, it mainly deals with the intimate connection between the Lord's resurrection and the resurrection of His body, the church (vs. 12-23) and the means by which this will happen (vs. 35-57).

1 Corinthians 15:12-23

"Now if Christ is preached that He has been raised from the dead, how do some among you say that there is no resurrection of the dead? (13) But if there is no resurrection of the dead, then Christ is not risen. (14) And if Christ is not risen, then our preaching is empty and your faith is also empty. (15) Yes, and we are found false witnesses of God, because we have testified of God that He raised up Christ, whom He did not raise up—if in fact the dead do not rise. (16) For if the dead do not rise, then Christ is not risen. (17) And if Christ is not risen, your faith is futile; you are still in your sins! (18) Then also those who have

fallen asleep in Christ have perished. (19) If in this life only we have hope in Christ, we are of all men the most pitiable.

(20) But now Christ is risen from the dead, and has become the firstfruits of those who have fallen asleep. (21) For since by man came death, by Man also came the resurrection of the dead. (22) For as in Adam all die, even so in Christ all shall be made alive. (23) But each one in his own order: Christ the firstfruits, afterward those who are Christ's at His coming."

Christ is the Firstfruits in Resurrection, the Believer will follow

This passage establishes a direct relationship between Christ having been raised from the dead and the future raising up of all believers in Christ. The future event is made *dependent* on the fact that Christ is already raised. He has become the firstfruits of all those who are His. Now doesn't this make sense? If Christ was raised from the dead and now is in a glorified body, it stands to reason that all those in Christ will be brought to glory in exactly the same way. It is not simply a reasonable assumption, but a dependent truth – because Christ was raised, we must be raised as well. There are two scriptural labels for Christ that reveal this truth.

1) **Firstfruits** – Christ is the firstfruits in resurrection and the glorification of the body. When He was raised from the dead, His 40 days and numerous appearances showed the disciples what a glorified Man would be like. He is the firstfruits – the word itself has the sense of prefiguring. (I Cor. 15:20, 23)

2) **Forerunner** – Christ, as the forerunner, has entered into the Presence behind the veil (Heb. 6:19-20). He is now there and our sure and steadfast hope enters there where He is. The words of Hebrews 6 are specific – He is the forerunner for us (the believer). This word also has the sense of prefiguring.

It should be the obvious conclusion, from these readings and the two labels, that Christ did none of this for Himself. His reasoning and motivation was all on our behalf.[6] He truly did not benefit from all this work, but it was all for us. It was so He could bring many sons to glory (Heb. 2:10). The believer is the beneficiary.

Christ's Redemptive Work was all for the Believer

If Christ is not raised, our faith is futile and worthless. If He is not risen, we have no confidence that our sins have been dealt with by God. If Christ has not been raised, then those who have fallen asleep have perished (I Cor. 15:17-18).

Romans 4:24-25

"...but also for us. It shall be imputed to us who believe in Him who raised up Jesus our Lord from the dead, who was delivered up because of our offenses, and was raised because of our justification."

He did all this for the believer. We are imputed righteous through our faith in the God who raised Christ up from among the dead. We have become the righteousness of God because Jesus Christ was made to be sin for us (II Cor. 5:21). He, who had no sin of His own, bore the sins of many (Heb. 9:28). He was delivered up for the believer's sins and iniquities, but resurrected on account of our justification. Through His death the Son of Man has accomplished a wonderful work in redemption on our behalf. It is the foundational work by which God, in all His plans and counsels, shows exceeding riches of grace in His kindness toward us in Christ Jesus (Eph. 2:7).

Immortality and Incorruptibility

1 Corinthians 15:47-56

(47) "The first man was of the earth, made of dust; the second Man is the Lord from heaven. (48) As was the man of dust, so also are those who are made of dust; and as is the heavenly Man, so also are those who are heavenly. (49) And as we have

borne the image of the man of dust, we shall also bear the image of the heavenly Man."

(50) "Now this I say, brethren, that flesh and blood cannot inherit the kingdom of God; nor does corruption inherit incorruption. (51) Behold, I tell you a mystery: We shall not all sleep, but we shall all be changed— (52) in a moment, in the twinkling of an eye, at the last trumpet. For the trumpet will sound, and the dead will be raised incorruptible, and we shall be changed. (53) For this corruptible must put on incorruption, and this mortal must put on immortality. (54) So when this corruptible has put on incorruption, and this mortal has put on immortality, then shall be brought to pass the saying that is written: "Death is swallowed up in victory."

(55) "O Death, where is your sting?
O Hades, where is your victory?"

(56) The sting of death is sin, and the strength of sin is the law."

This is the other promised passage that gives much detail concerning the rapture. For the church it is immortality and incorruptibility through the removal of sin from the flesh. With this there is the total defeat of death and the power of death against us (Rom. 5:12). We know that Satan has been defeated already, that the prince of the world had been cast out by the work of the cross (John 12:31). The Son of Man went down under death so that He might destroy him who had the power of death, the devil. This has already been accomplished (Heb. 2:14). However, we see in this passage that the rapture of the church is the bringing out, by the sovereign power of God, the final details of our redemption – the glorification of our bodies.[7] Sin will have been removed and death will no longer be able to touch any of those in Christ.

In this passage we also see the heavenly connection with the second Man from heaven (v.47). Believers are those with a heavenly calling and citizenship, who are heavenly, and will bear the image of the heavenly Man (vs. 48-49). In the above account of this blessed event we have the same final trumpet call that is found in I Thess. 4:16, as well as the dead in Christ resurrected and the remaining being changed (vs. 51-53). All these verses describe the same details of the rapture that we found before. It is the blessed hope of the church.

Chapter 2: Endnotes

[5] In the Christian world there are many who, for various reasons, do not believe in the doctrine of the rapture of the church. In this chapter I deal with the human thought that we must add to the detailed description of this event a U-turn and a remaining on the earth of all involved. It is not that this group would argue with the biblical description of the event as it is found in the scriptures, but simply they add to it in order to keep us on the earth and effectively deny the believer's heavenly calling. Other groups of naysayers argue with the timing of the rapture. This I address in later chapters.

[6] Those who are taught of scripture will realize that the Son of Man coming from heaven was intensely motivated to be obedient to do God's will, which is specifically defined as His death (please read Heb. 10:1-14). In this passage, God's will was the need for a sacrifice that would be pleasing to Him. A pleasing sacrifice is one that would satisfy all God's holy and righteous claims justly held by God against man, because of the presence of sin in the flesh and the committing of sins. This sacrifice, which obviously implies the death of the victim, would glorify God – a propitiation to perfectly satisfy these claims. This sacrifice being perfect would be a one-time and eternal sacrifice. But obviously in His coming, a body prepared for Him, His motivation was "to do Your will, O God." In the text of the chapter I was emphasizing those who benefited from this work of redemption – the believer/church. Obviously the Lord was motivated, not only to glorify God, but to eventually see the fruit of His travail/labors, the many sons to be brought to glory.

[7] This is a principle found in different situations throughout the Word of God. It is seen in having a spiritual truth in title and possession, yet in God's timing having to wait for its complete and full reality, often in a physical way. A great example of this principle is seen in I John 3:2. Here John says, *"...now we are children of God; and it has not yet been revealed what we shall be, but we know that when He is revealed, we shall be like Him..."* It is now we are, but later we shall be. We have eternal life now and are fully children of God. Later on, in all believers, this same life will swallow up both corruptibility and mortality, depending on which state you are found in at the time of the rapture.

This same principle can be found in many of the judgments of God. A great example of this is found in John 12:31 – the judgment of both the world and Satan. Presently it is an accomplished fact and truth in the cross. The devil, holding the power of death, has been destroyed by the death and cross of Christ (Heb. 2:14). His defeat and destruction is held in title presently and we, as believers, should say he is a defeated devil that we simply resist in faith. But his physical judgment will be in the future like this:

1.) He will be thrown out of the heavens and down to the earth with three and a half years remaining (Rev. 12:7-12). On the earth he has great wrath for his time is short.

2.) After the defeat of the Roman beast, the Antichrist, and all the armies of man at Christ's physical return to this earth, Satan will be bound in a bottomless pit for 1000 years (Rev. 20:1-3).

3.) After the 1000 years he will be released for one final temptation of man on earth. This rebellion is destroyed and the devil is cast into the lake of fire, tormented forever and ever (Rev. 20:7-10).

The same principle is found in the judgment of the world. Its judgment was declared and accomplished with the lifting up of the Son of Man from the earth on the cross. Jesus said at that time, "Now is the judgment of this world." Its physical judgment will be accomplished later, when Christ physically returns to this earth and during His kingdom (II Tim. 4:1). The judgment of the living is by the Son of Man at His appearing. The judgment of the dead is at the end of the earthly kingdom of the Son of Man, at the end of the 1000 year millennium (Rev. 20:11-15). But for the believer in faith, our relationship with the world is over, and we are not of the world (Col. 2:20, Gal. 6:14) – this is a separate biblical principle and truth. However, when you bring these two principles together, you get another biblical truth that many people have a hard time seeing.

- The world is judged and condemned in the time of Christ and His cross. The book of Revelation, from chapter four and beyond, depicts the physical judgment of the wicked world and all that is part of it.

- When the Son of Man was lifted up from the earth, Jesus said that we are not of the world as He is not of the world (John 15:19, 17:14).

When these two principles are combined should be easy to see. Why would God leave us on the earth during His judgment of this world, if in fact we are not of the world in the same manner that Jesus is not of the world?

Notes

Chapter 3:

The Exceeding Greatness of His Power

The removal of the church from this earth will be an awesome physical display of God's sovereign power and grace. It will be expressly and exclusively the work of God. It will be the end of our salvation, the finalizing of the believer's redemption, and our entrance into the very glory of God. Jesus Christ will descend from heaven to gather up His brethren in order to bring the many sons to glory. God's power in life will swallow up mortality. God's power in resurrection will raise the dead in Christ. It will be the beginnings of the realization of all our Biblical hopes and promises.

This future event was prefigured in the raising and exalting of Jesus Christ from the dead and to the right hand of God. The same power that will be used on behalf of the church has already been demonstrated and displayed.

Ephesians 1:17-20

(17) "that the God of our Lord Jesus Christ, the Father of glory, may give to you the spirit of wisdom and revelation in the knowledge of Him, (18) the eyes of your understanding being

enlightened; that you may know what is the hope of His calling, what are the riches of the glory of His inheritance in the saints, (19) and what is the exceeding greatness of His power toward us who believe, according to the working of His mighty power (20) which He worked in Christ when He raised Him from the dead and seated Him at His right hand in the heavenly places"

Paul's desire in this prayer is for believers to receive an understanding and knowledge of the Father of glory. He is the God of our Lord Jesus Christ – a statement that in some ways may seem strange, but its understanding brings enlightenment and blessing. When Jesus was raised from the grave He said this, *"I am ascending to my Father and your Father, and to My God and your God."* The word 'God,' used here, establishes that Jesus Christ bore the title of the Son of Man, and by His obedience to death fully glorified God (John 13:31-32). God in turn would glorify the Son of Man. However, the use of the name 'Father' establishes the truth that Jesus Christ is the Son of God.

The Son of God was sent by the Father

The Son of God revealed the Father. The Son's obedience was such that He only spoke the words the Father gave Him to speak (John 12:49-50), He only did the works He saw His Father doing (John 5:20, 36, 10:32, 37-38). The Son willingly chose to be a servant to the Father's will, and never considered doing His own (John 5:30, 6:38). If you saw the Son, you had seen the Father (John 12:45, 14:7-11). He would say, "I and my Father are one..." and, "...I am in the Father, and the Father in Me." The Son came into this world, taking on human flesh, and walked with the Father in Him, therefore perfectly revealing the Father.

In this revelation of the Father by the Son our eyes and understanding behold a beautiful relationship that goes beyond the words spoken and the works done. It is that which exists between the Father and the Son and the Son with the Father. When the Son came, He revealed the name of God as that of 'Father' – at least one of the distinct persons of the Godhead. And always in our view is the intimate relationship between the Father and the Son.

When Philip asked, *"Lord, show us the Father,"* He answered by saying, *"Have I been with you so long, and yet you have not known Me…how can you say, 'Show us the Father'?"* You have to sense the disappointment in His words. They all had failed to realize the relationship between the Son and the Father. He told them that from now on you know the Father and have seen Him. But this they had failed to see and comprehend – the intimate relationship between Father and Son, and how He perfectly showed this and revealed it. With their failure to have eyes to see in faith and in His disappointment, He falls back on the proof of the words and works (John 14:10-11). He finally says, *"…or else believe Me for the sake of the works themselves."*

No doubt the Lord was disappointed by their lack of spiritual perception and faith. However He knew the time was soon coming when they would fully understand this relationship, and the revelation of the Father.

The Holy Spirit – the Spirit of Truth

John 16:25

"These things I have spoken to you in figurative language; but the time is coming when I will no longer speak to you in figurative language, but I will tell you plainly about the Father."

In all this discourse He has during His last night with His disciples, when He uses a phrase like 'the time is coming' He is referring to when the Holy Spirit would be sent down, after He departed from them and was glorified (John 7:38-39). The Holy Spirit dwelling in them from the day of Pentecost, being the Spirit of truth, would lead and guide them into all the truth about the Father. It would include a full understanding of the relationship of the Son and the many sons with the Father. This is where Jesus was taking them in their understanding, but where they fell short not having the Spirit as yet. However, because you are sons and for the purpose of the knowledge of this relationship, God has sent forth the Spirit of His Son into your hearts, crying out, "Abba Father!"[8]

In Paul's prayer in Ephesians 1 the knowledge of the Father is what is sought by wisdom and revelation of the Holy Spirit. He points to the hope of God's calling upon the believer and the richness of the inheritance that the Father will give the many sons with Christ. The believer is an heir of the Father and a co-heir with the Son of God – *"Therefore you are no longer a slave but a son, and if a son, then an heir of God through Christ."* (Gal. 4:7) It is the Father who gives the inheritance to the sons. God's calling of the believer is heavenly (Heb. 3:1). Peter tells us the inheritance for the saints is laid up in heaven. It is in the heavenly places where the Father blesses us with every spiritual blessing, which will be the exceeding riches of His grace in His kindness towards the church throughout the ages to come (Eph. 1:3, 2:7).

The church, the body of Christ, is presently seated in heavenly places in Christ (Eph. 2:6). It was Jesus as the Head with the body that was exalted above all principality and power (Eph. 1:21-23). It is a position the body holds mostly in title now, in this present age. Professing Christianity on the earth, through the passing of time and by its multiplied failures in responsibility, has lost what blessing and privilege this positioning once gave. Much could be said and written on this particular subject, so much that it would fill a book. But I will give you one thought to consider here. It seems conclusive to me that in the testimony of Scripture concerning Christendom on earth, that God does not presently recognize and acknowledge it as a corporate entity.[9] [Please read the chapter endnote #8 explaining this thought.]

What man builds on the earth with wood, hay, and stubble will not, in any way, affect the sovereign work of God. Jesus said, *"...I will build My church..."* This He does as His own work. And further, *"...the gates of Hades will not prevail against it."* This is the work of God alone, which cannot and will not fail.

The Resurrection of Jesus Christ prefigures the Rapture

In His own timing, when the 'fullness of the Gentiles' comes in (Rom. 11:25) He will remove the body of Christ from this earth and world. This also will be the sovereign work of God, a work made without hands. It will be one of the greatest displays of God's sovereign power and grace.

Ephesians 1:19-20 (Amplified Bible)

"And so that you can know and understand what is the immeasurable and unlimited and surpassing greatness of His power in and for us who believe, as demonstrated in the working of His mighty strength,

Which He exerted in Christ when He raised Him from the dead and seated Him at His own right hand in the heavenly places,"

God raising Christ from the dead was a demonstration, a display, and in many ways a prefiguring of the event that will be the physical display of the exceeding greatness of His power towards us who believe. This event is yet to come; Christ raised up from among the dead is an accomplished fact. The scriptures speak, "But now Christ is risen from the dead, and has become the firstfruits of those who have fallen asleep." This is a prefiguring. Again, "...the Presence behind the veil, where the forerunner has entered for us, even Jesus..." is a prefiguring. When the NKJV uses the phrase 'according to the working of His mighty power' it is the sense of a demonstration that prefigures a future event. The entire passage is presented with the emphasis on what God does 'toward us who believe.'

The exceeding greatness of His Power

And what are the full results?

Ephesians 1:19-23

(19) "and what is the exceeding greatness of His power toward us who believe, according to the working of His mighty power (20) which He worked in Christ when He raised Him from the dead and seated Him at His right hand in the heavenly places, (21) far above all principality and power and might and dominion, and every name that is named, not only in this age but also in that which is to come.

(22) And He put all things under His feet, and gave Him to be head over all things to the church, (21) which is His body, the fullness of Him who fills all in all."

The body of Christ will be raised as Christ was raised, by the same awesome power of God. The whole church will be changed, having glorified bodies like His. It will be, in a great sense, the church's physical union to the Head in the heavens after its departure from the earth. Christ is exalted far above all principality and power and might and dominion, and His body is not separated from Him in this. All things will be realized as put under the feet of His body, the church being the fullness of Christ, who fills all in all. The Father will give the inheritance to His many sons, and we will enjoy it throughout the ages to come with Christ and as His brethren.

Here is a review of how the main passages of this doctrine are connected and support each other.

- In I Corinthians 15 – Christ is now raised from the dead, and so we must be raised and/or glorified in body just as He is.

- I Thessalonians 4 – we will be caught up, the Lord personally coming for us, forever to be with Him in the glorified state.

- John 14 – He comes back for us to take us where He was, into the presence of the Father in the heavens.

- Ephesians 1:17-23 – the exceeding great power of God will raise up and glorify the church, His body, to His right hand in glory, far above all things created.

This doctrine teaches, from a sound scriptural basis and by sound Biblical principles, the rapture of the church. In this age, it is and always will be the blessed hope of the church.

Chapter 3: Endnotes

[8] During the Lord's last discourse with the disciples before His departure, He spoke of both the Father and Himself sending the Holy Spirit. This sending of the Spirit by the Father concerns the relationship of sonship being established. When one is drawn to faith in Christ and believes in His shed blood, he receives eternal life. Having believed, he will then be sealed by the seal of the Spirit from the Father (Eph. 1:13). As given by the Father it is the Spirit of sonship, the Spirit of His Son sent forth into our hearts, crying out, "Abba, Father!" According to His purpose and in this character, the believer learns the intimate dealings, blessings, and affections of his now established relationship with the Father, as well as the inheritance He gives to His sons. This is why God is not Father to the world, nor is He to the Jews (John 8:42, 54-55), because the Spirit as sent by the Father, the world simply cannot receive, because it neither sees Him nor knows Him (John 14:16-17).

[9] The history of the failure of Christendom when responsibility was placed in man's hands is well documented, even as seen and predicted in scripture. Paul was given the responsibility for laying the foundation for the building of the church on the earth, "According to the grace of God given to me, as a wise master builder I have laid the foundation..." (I Cor. 3:10-11) Please note; it was not Peter, James, or John that were given this stewardship. The apostle Paul was the chosen vessel by God specifically given this dispensation concerning the mystery, the church on earth (Eph. 3:1-9). It was his stewardship to reveal the mystery, teach the doctrine of the church, and lay its foundation responsibly.

But others build on the foundation; ministers placed in corporate responsibility in the church world. The exhortation is, "But let each one take heed how he builds on it." What has been the history – that is, the building on the earth by man in responsibility? In Paul's time the mystery of lawlessness was already at work in the church (II Thess. 2:7). But most telling are his final words to the Ephesian elders before departing for Jerusalem – words that directly reference the failure of responsibility in the administration and government in the church after Paul's death. *(Acts 20:28-31)*

"Therefore take heed to yourselves and to all the flock, among which the Holy Spirit has made you overseers, to shepherd the church of God which He purchased with His own blood. For I know

this, that after my departure savage wolves will come in among you, not sparing the flock. Also from among yourselves men will rise up, speaking perverse things, to draw away the disciples after themselves. Therefore watch, and remember that for three years I did not cease to warn everyone night and day with tears."

The infiltration of evil and corruption was already present in the early apostolic church. Its history would be its growth and ripening until eventually all God's restraint on it is lifted. Before the end there will come forth one final great apostasy in the church world (II Thess. 2:3). There is more testimony from scripture that could be given on this history, but this should suffice to impress the point.

Jehovah once dwelt in the midst of Israel, behind the veil in the tabernacle and in Solomon's temple. However, the glory could never be found in Nehemiah's rebuilt temple. Why? Solomon failed in responsibility as the son of David, the kingdom was divided, and idolatry and apostasy ran rampant. God could no longer tolerate Israel's sin and His presence and glory left the earth. The Jewish people were no longer recognized or acknowledged by Jehovah. They were not His people, and He was not their God (Hosea 1:9). This is a lesson well worth understanding, for no doubt it has been repeated in Christendom.

Notes

Chapter 4:
The Image of His Son

The counsels of God represent all the work God will do on behalf of all creation. Certain parts of His counsels preceded the creation of the world. These counsels spring forth from God's own will. His will is the cause of, or results in, the decisions and choices He makes. The purpose of His will is directly reflected by His choices and decisions. God has always had a plan, and when He works, it is always according to His plan. As the sovereign God He simply works 'all things.' This does not mean that He is the direct agent of everything that takes place, but rather that nothing escapes Him. Nothing can happen, nor does happen, that does not fit into His overall plan. This would have to include the general as well as the specific, the good as well as the evil – if God is sovereign, then nothing escapes Him or is outside His plan. God exercises an active control and oversight over all things and all events.[10]

Ephesians 1:11

"In Him also we have obtained an inheritance, being predestined according to the purpose of Him who works all things according to the counsel of His will,"

The Counsels of God – the specific purpose of His will

This verse gives credibility to the general statements I made preceding it above. An additional truth of specific detail is evident from this verse – that 'in Christ' the believer has been made or enabled to obtain an inheritance from God. The giving of this inheritance is seen as to certain ones (we) before the creation of the world. These are all true believers being made acceptable to God, as they are found 'in the Beloved' Son (Eph. 1:6). This 'acceptance' by God of certain ones in the Beloved also preceded the foundations of the world (Eph. 1:4-5).

All these verses in the first half of Ephesians 1 help to establish certain spiritual truths and realities.

1) God's counsel and plan exists according to the purpose of His will – His choices and decisions are of His will and therefore reflect the purpose of His will.

2) God is sovereign and therefore works all things. As God's word cannot return to Him 'void,' neither can His counsel (Is. 55:11).

3) Certain parts of His counsel were determined before the world was created. This is part of the meaning of the word 'predestined' in Ephesians 1:5 and Ephesians 1:11.

4) In the first half of Ephesians 1 there are two things definitely seen as before the foundation of the world – the inheritance given in title to the believer (v. 11) and the complete and absolute acceptance by God of the believer in His Beloved Son, Jesus Christ (vs. 3-7).

The Counsels of God before the Foundation of the World

Now with these understandings from the scriptures, we will look at a similar passage in the epistle to the Romans.

Romans 8:29-30

(29) "For whom He foreknew, He also predestined to be conformed to the image of His Son, that He might be the firstborn among many brethren. (30) Moreover whom He predestined, these He also called; whom He called, these He also justified; and whom He justified, these He also glorified."

The passage is speaking of the counsel and plan of God. It speaks of the believer in Christ and the sovereign work of God on his behalf. With the use of such words as 'foreknew' and 'predestined' we know the Spirit is speaking of the parts of God's counsel that existed before creation, before the world existed. What is interesting are the five prominent words in this passage and the need for our correct understanding and perceptions concerning how they are used.

1. **Foreknew** – the predetermined counsel of God before the foundations of the world.

2. **Predestined** – the choice of God in His predetermined counsel.

3. **Called** – the beginning of the work of God in drawing and separating unto Himself. It is based upon His previous choice and is always without repentance – He never has to change His mind or have an alternate selection ready. That would simply be unnecessary and contrary to any proper understanding of God's sovereignty.

4. **Justified** – God becomes the justifier of those who have faith in Jesus; a faith in His death and blood. God's righteousness was satisfied and demonstrated in Christ being made sin and bearing sins, His blood being the propitiation (Rom. 3:24-26). God has justified all those in Christ, freely by His grace, through the redemptive death of Christ. God raising Christ out of death represents the already accomplished truth of the believer justified by God. Jesus was raised because of our justification (Rom. 5:25).

5. **Glorified** – the believer will be clothed in a heavenly body, a building from God (II Cor. 5:1-2). We will all be changed (those in Christ) – I Cor. 15:51. This will be either resurrection from the dead, or life swallowing up the mortality of the earthly body.

Each of these words is used in the past tense in the passage. In the mind of God His counsels are already accomplished. Certainly Jesus came to this earth at a given point in time, but He was the Lamb slain from the foundation of the world. When He was raised from the dead, the believer was already justified. For the believer, only one of these remains yet future – the glorified body. However, as we can see, it is as good as done. If it is God's counsel, then there can be no question about it. As is the testimony here, those God justified, these He also glorified.

Conformed to the Image of His Son

This passage makes it decidedly the counsel of God – He is the one who foreknew us, and He is the one who predestined us. And for what purpose? *God's counsel is for every believer to be conformed to the image of His Son.* This directly refers to the glorifying of the believer, the glorifying of our bodies. It will be the time of the rapture of the church. All that remains from this list of five above is for the believer's body to be conformed to be like Christ.

The list of five words in the above passage describes the sovereign grace and work of God in accomplishing the redemption of the believer. It is God's work, it is God's will, and it shows here how it is actually and entirely God's decision. This is the sovereignty of God and it speaks of the only way redemption is accomplished. It is easy to see that there is no human involvement at all in the list. That is because there is no human involvement in the redemption of the believer. All believers are His workmanship, created in Christ Jesus, and for His glory. God alone will be the One who will conform every believer into the image of His Son.

Now if we want to pervert the teaching of the passage we will add in human thoughts and human efforts. We will say the 'conforming to the image of His Son' is sanctification. The problem is the word 'sanctification' didn't make the list. And this is for good reason. The phrase 'conformed to the image of His Son' refers to the word 'predestined' – the expression of the purpose and will of God as decided by Him before the foundations of the world. The word predestined comes before the words 'called' and 'justified.' How would the thought of sanctification fit there? It wouldn't! Further, believers conformed to the image of His Son is for a definite reason – so that Christ might be the firstborn among the many brethren. Firstborn? Yes – Christ is the firstborn from among the dead (Rev. 1:5, I Cor. 15:20, 23). It is evident and obvious that since we are to be conformed to the image of our Lord Jesus, *it must be by way of resurrection and by glorification.* Why? *Because He is the firstborn as risen and glorified!* And this, for the believer, will be the rapture of the church and alone the work of God.

Sanctification – for our walk of Faith on this Earth

There is a present work of God's grace that goes on within every believer as we walk upon this earth and in this world. It is a work of grace in us that we can properly call 'sanctification.'

John 17:14-17

(14) "I have given them Your word; and the world has hated them because they are not of the world, just as I am not of the world. (15) I do not pray that You should take them out of the world, but that You should keep them from the evil one. (16) They are not of the world, just as I am not of the world. (17) Sanctify them by Your truth. Your word is truth."

This is the progressive working of God's grace in the believer. It is the washing of the water of the Word of God. Jesus gave us the Father's word and by it He keeps us from the evil in this world. This is what we should be experiencing in our walks – a real setting apart from the world around us. Sanctify them by Your word. As He said concerning the disciples at that time in John 15:3, *"You are already clean because of the word which I have spoken to you."*

2 Corinthians 3:18

"But we all, with unveiled face, beholding as in a mirror the glory of the Lord, are being transformed into the same image from glory to glory, just as by the Spirit of the Lord."

Again, this is our present experience. The mirror is the Word of God. When we are taught by the Spirit in His Word, we behold a Christ in glory. It is this image we are progressively changed into, from glory to glory. But on this earth and in this world we never stop walking as believers. If we do we effectively join to the world in our experience. As our High Priest, Jesus never stops washing our feet, for this world is defilement for us as we walk around in it (John 13:7). And while we are here we can never say we have already attained, or are already perfected (Phil. 3:12), because sin remains in the flesh. We are progressively changed, being transformed into the image of a Christ in glory. However, none of us can count ourselves as having apprehended yet, but we press on (Phil. 3:13).

The Believer's Glorified Body

Yet we know we will be perfectly like Him. The Father desires that all the brethren be conformed to the image of His Son. *This will not be a progressive work of grace in the believer on this earth*, but rather the display of His exceeding great power, in the twinkling of an eye, and a catching away from this world. He has already made provision for this.

2 Corinthians 5:4-5

"For we who are in this tent groan, being burdened, not because we want to be unclothed, but further clothed, that mortality may be swallowed up by life. Now He who has prepared us for this very thing is God, who also has given us the Spirit as a guarantee."

God has prepared the believer for this very thing, the glorifying of our bodies. He has given us the Spirit to dwell in us. This same Spirit is our guarantee of all our proper hopes, which is not to be unclothed, but further clothed and to enter into glory. The Father has sealed us with the Spirit of sonship (Rom. 8:15-17).

Romans 8:11

"But if the Spirit of Him who raised Jesus from the dead dwells in you, He who raised Christ from the dead will also give life to your mortal bodies through His Spirit who dwells in you."

This is the glorification of the believer. And it is purely a Christian thing – the result of the presence of His Spirit dwelling in you. It defines what the scriptures refer to as the resurrection of the just. It will be what occurs at the rapture of the church, for the body of Christ is individual members one of another, united corporately by the Spirit.

The Blessed Hope of the Believer

Romans 8:23-25

(23) "Not only that, but we also who have the firstfruits of the Spirit, even we ourselves groan within ourselves, eagerly waiting for the adoption, the redemption of our body. (24) For we were saved in this hope, but hope that is seen is not hope; for why does one still hope for what he sees? (25) But if we hope for what we do not see, we eagerly wait for it with perseverance."

As believers, having the indwelling Holy Spirit as the guarantee, we eagerly wait for the redemption of our bodies. In our present earthly bodies we groan, a type of intercession and longing, looking forward in a sure anticipation for what God will do for us. *"For in this we groan, earnestly desiring to be clothed with our habitation which is from heaven...for we who are in this tent groan, being burdened..."* (II Cor. 5:2-4).

We are presently saved. We possess eternal life. We are now sons of God, and have the seal of the Spirit. But it is clear we were saved (past tense) in this hope (the future glorifying of our bodies). All our proper hopes, as believers, remain to be fulfilled when our bodies are redeemed. And our Christian hopes remain unseen, for they are not of this present time, nor during this present life on the earth (Rom. 8:18).[11] Nevertheless, they are true and certain hopes given to us in promise from our faithful God and Father. It is a sure and steadfast hope, an anchor of the believer's soul, which enters into the Presence where the forerunner has gone already (Heb. 6:19-20).

Philippians 3:20-21

For our citizenship is in heaven, from which we also eagerly wait for the Savior, the Lord Jesus Christ, who will transform our lowly body that it may be conformed to His glorious body, according to the working by which He is able even to subdue all things to Himself.

The believer's home is in heaven. It is from there that we eagerly look for our Lord to appear from and to take us there. It is where our Father is. We are to live as sons in the house of the Father. The Lord is coming for us to take us to Him. At that time our lowly earthly bodies must be changed. When we are glorified, our bodies are transformed into the image of His glorious body. It is a hope that we eagerly wait for and earnestly desire. We will be conformed to the image of the Father's Beloved Son. It is accomplished already in God's mind. The Spirit expressly testifies, *"...and whom He justified, these He also glorified."* This is the blessed hope of the believer and the blessed hope of the church.

Chapter 4: Endnotes

[10] God is never the direct cause or agent of evil. God is holy and righteous in nature and character. It would be impossible for God to be guilty of such. He is holy and by definition hates evil and sin. He is righteous and by definition always deals justly when He deals directly with man. Men often point an accusing finger at God, but His direct or indirect judgments are always righteous. God will never compromise His own nature in anything that He does, always remaining true to Himself. All His acts and judgments are righteous dealings and serve to glorify Him.

God is sovereign, and although He is never the direct agent of evil, He will use evil men to accomplish His own purposes and plans. The Assyrian, Nebuchadnezzar, and the Romans were all used by God as a rod of judgment and correction. Pharaoh was humbled by His direct judgments so that the name of Jehovah would be declared in all the earth.

The principle of this present time is the goodness and grace of God in the gospel of Jesus Christ. By the preaching of the gospel to every creature, those who believe will be saved, and those who do not believe will be condemned (Mark 16:15-16). Please take note: this is an individual thing. Israel as a people and a nation are set aside presently by God. The principle in operation during the gathering of the church is not God dealing with nations on the earth. The principle of the gospel does not have this character. Israel will not be saved by the gospel and neither will America. At the present time the Son of Man sits at the right hand of God, hidden from the world. Consequent to this, the Holy Spirit has been sent down to gather in the body of Christ. When the fullness of the Gentiles is gathered in, God will remove the body from the earth. Then you will see the power of God in His judgment of evil on this earth and in this world. Then you will see God dealing with nations, and the first one will be Israel.

We would do well to trace the principle of evil through the history of man in scripture. *"Therefore, just as through one man sin entered the world, and death through sin, and thus death spread to all men, because all sinned."* (Rom. 5:12) When man was chased from the garden, he entered the world and spread sin all around. In principle evil grew and filled the earth and God could no longer tolerate it. He righteously judged and destroyed it. After the flood, Satan introduces idolatry into the world as a new form of evil, filling the earth. The world continues in its principles of sin and evil. Satan is the god and prince of this present evil age.

As for Israel as a chosen nation, delivered from the world (Egypt) in type by the power of God and brought before Him at Mt. Sinai, they did not fare much better. Immediately they made the golden calf. Also many were judged by God for their sin and evil, dying in the wilderness. When God brought them into the land they eventually set up idols in high places and committed apostasy. God chastised the nation in many ways and by His prophets tried to call Israel back to His law. But man in the flesh cannot please God. Eventually the presence of God left the nation of Israel, and the city and temple were destroyed. The unclean spirit of idolatry was delivered from Israel by their captivity in Babylon. This spirit now travels through dry places, seeking rest, but finding none. It will return to the house from which it came, only with seven other spirits more wicked than itself. This house is Israel under the Antichrist in the end. Then last of all God sent His Son to them, saying, 'They will respect my Son.' They cast Him out and killed Him (Matt. 21:37-39). Evil in principle has grown and flourished in Israel in many ways and in many different sins.

In the cross, both the world and Israel rejected God. He came into this world in goodness and grace, but only received hatred for it (John 15:22-25). In His humiliation, He walked as a suffering servant, always showing compassion and grace, and loving His own who were in the world, He loved them to the end (John 13:1). Our portion as believers, on the earth and in this world presently, is to walk as He walked and to love one another as He loved us (John 15:12-13). In His humiliation He did not reign as a King. Neither will the true believer reign as a king in life at this present time. The principle of this present age for the believer's portion is to suffer with Christ, so that in the coming age we may be glorified together. The Lord tells us that in the world you will have tribulation and that the world will hate us because we are not of them (John 16:33, 17:14, 15:19 and II Tim. 3:10-12).

What about the principle of evil in the church world? In Paul's lifetime the testimony of the Spirit was that the mystery of lawlessness was already at work! Early on evil had a foothold through the lack of responsibility in the corporate body (II Thess. 2:7). It has been growing and ripening to full fruit ever since. (Please see: II Tim. 3:1-5, 3:13, 4:3-4, I Tim. 4:1-2, I John 2:18-19, 4:3-5, II Peter 2:1-2, Jude 3-8) Ephesus never returned to its first state and position, and the church world has been on a path of steady decline and decay. More scripture could be referenced, more examples could be given, but this is suffice to prove that the principle of evil was present early on in Christendom and did well and prospered.

As Sovereign, God at this time restricts evil in the world. He only allows it to go so far. But this is not the time in which God will use His power and righteously judge this world. That time is yet to come. Presently, it often looks like evil and the wicked prosper in this world. Again, the principle toward this world at this time is goodness and grace from God, not judgment. At this time God hinders the full expression of evil in the church world (II Thess. 2:6-7). When this restraining comes to an end there will be a great apostasy in Christendom, after which the man of sin comes forth (II Thess. 2:3). The apostasy will result from the body of Christ being removed from the earth in the rapture. The evil and corrupt condition of the professing church world is seen symbolically in Thyatira, Sardis, Laodicea, and the great harlot of Revelation 17-18. It will be judged and destroyed first, before God turns to judge the world (I Peter 4:17).

In the coming dispensation the principles will be different. By the return of the Son of Man to this earth, God will righteously judge and destroy the present evil, rebellion, and apostasy of the world. Jesus will take up His power and by it destroy all the civil power and influence brought on the face of the earth through the four great Gentile dynasties (Dan. 2:31-35), "...so that no trace of them was found." Satan will be bound in the bottomless pit for 1000 years. It is only after this initial judgment of the present evil that the 'stone' that struck the image became a great mountain and filled the whole earth. During the millennium, the Son of Man will rule all nations with a rod of iron (Rev. 12:5, 2:26-27, Ps. 2:6-9). The use of His power in the righteous judgment of evil and sin is how the glory of God will fill the entire earth. At the end of this dispensation the Son of Man will judge the wicked dead at the great white throne. This is the resurrection of the wicked as distinguished from the resurrection of the just in scriptures. All at the great white throne are cast into the lake of fire, as is Satan. The lake of fire is God's final and eternal location for all evil judged. All the living that remain on the earth at the end of the 1000 year dispensation will be glorified, sin being removed from their flesh.

What follows this is the new heavens and earth. Here the principles are different as well. All sin will have been removed from the flesh, and all evil and wickedness contained in the lake of fire. Evil and sin will not exist in the eternal state. There will be no need for a reign of power in righteous judgment, but rather it will be a state wherein righteousness dwells and God is all in all in His divine eternal glory.

This has been a short discussion of the principle of sin and evil as it is found in Scripture and in the history of man. It has also been a discussion of differing Biblical principles established at certain periods of time by which the sovereign God deals with evil. Without understanding the general principles, the believer will not comprehend the overall plan and counsel of God. When one grasps these general principles, then the detail of scripture and prophecy is made easier to understand.

One last point: At the end of this present age there will be a time of the greatest display of evil ever known to man on the face of the earth (Mark 13:19). It is the three and a half years that precede the return of Christ to this earth. These years are known in scripture as Jacob's trouble (Jer. 30:7, Dan. 12:1) and the great tribulation (Matt. 24:21-22). The body of Christ will have previously been removed from the earth by which the remaining tares of professing Christianity will apostatize. The great dragon will be cast out of the heavens down to the earth. It will be, "Woe to the inhabitants of the earth and the sea! For the devil has come down to you, having great wrath (Rev. 12:12), because he knows that he has a short time." The character of the dragon on the earth, as well as the two beasts of Revelation 13 at this time, is open rebellion, apostasy, blasphemy, and idolatry. The Jewish people will be seven times worse than the nation was in the time of Elijah and the prophets of Baal. God will have removed His restraint of evil so that 'the man of sin' could come forth. "The coming of the lawless one is according to the working of Satan, with all power, signs, and lying wonders, and with all unrighteous deception...for this reason God will send them strong delusion, that they should believe the lie." (II Thess. 2:8-12)

[11] All proper Christian hopes are unseen. Hope that is seen is not hope at all. Therefore, there are no proper hopes for the believer in our walk presently on this earth. We have a walk of faith in this life. And we know this (Heb. 11:1), "...faith is the substance of things hoped for, the evidence of things not seen." All proper Christian hopes can only be found in glory. So we have, "...Christ in you, the hope of glory." Christian faith has three understandings or emphasizes:

1. Faith is in the God who raises the dead. This is the object of Christian faith – the God of resurrection (Rom. 4:23-24, II Cor. 1:9, Heb. 11:19, Rom. 10:9, I Pet. 1:21, Col. 2:12). This places the doctrine of the rapture, the resurrection of the church, as an integral part of Christian faith.

2. Faith is the substance of all our hopes, the evidence of the unseen (Heb. 11:1). The Christian's hopes are beyond this

present time and associated with the glory we will enter into (Rom. 5:2, Col. 1:27).

3. Presently, we walk by faith, while on this earth and in this world (II Cor. 5:7). By faith we endure hardships, afflictions, persecutions, hatred in the world. Presently we suffer with Christ (Rom. 8:17-18), and we are privileged to count it all joy to suffer for Him (Phil. 1:27-30). When we leave this world our walk by faith ends.

Notes

Chapter 5:

The Inheritance of the Saints

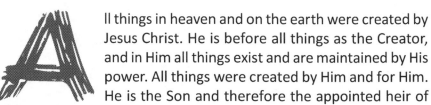ll things in heaven and on the earth were created by Jesus Christ. He is before all things as the Creator, and in Him all things exist and are maintained by His power. All things were created by Him and for Him. He is the Son and therefore the appointed heir of all which He created (Heb. 1:2). The inheritance is of all things, visible or invisible: thrones, dominions, principalities, and powers. It is all destined to be His.

Sin entered in and by it all creation became defiled. Whether it was the sin of Satan or that of Adam, defilement reached into the heavens, approaching the very throne of God. A reconciliation was needed, one that would be pure and perfect, and would appease the righteous and holy God. The reconciliation of all things in heaven and on earth, visible and invisible, was through the shed blood of Jesus Christ, the Son of Man.

Colossians 1:19-20

"For it pleased the Father that in Him all the fullness should dwell, and by Him to reconcile all things to Himself, by Him, whether things on earth or things in heaven, having made peace through the blood of His cross."

But this alone would not satisfy all the counsel of God. The Father would have a body for His glorified Son. He desired that there would be many children, many sons in His household. He would have a bride for His Son, an Eve to present to the second Adam after He awoke in glory.[12]

The Reconciliation of the Body of Christ

This body, of necessity, would need to be redeemed and reconciled. Man's disobedience in the garden was the cause of the corruption that spread upon all things (Rom. 8:19-21), but it also brought sin into man's flesh and death by its presence (Rom. 5:12). Man was lost and in ruin. He was alienated from God his Creator. He was banished from paradise, removed from the presence of God. By birth and by nature, man was a child of wrath. Redemption and reconciliation were desperately needed.

Colossians 1:21-22

"And you, who once were alienated and enemies in your mind by wicked works, yet now He has reconciled in the body of His flesh through death, to present you holy, and blameless, and above reproach in His sight."

It is true that all mankind was alienated and enemies of God, and that reconciliation for man must necessarily come through man, and so by the death of the Son of Man. This is a principle and understanding of great importance. Jesus was in the form of God and equal with God, for He was God. Yet He made Himself of no reputation, and came in the likeness of men.[13] This allowed Him to be able to humble Himself to the death of the cross (Phil. 2:5-8). So the redemption of man comes through the work of Jesus Christ, the Son of Man.

Certain scriptural truths proceed from this death. It should be abundantly clear it was the Son of Man that God raised from the dead (Matt. 17:9), and that a Man has now entered the glory of God (Luke 22:69, Heb. 10:12). Having said all this brings out this scriptural understanding – none of these things occurred for Him, for His personal benefit, or to further His own personal glory. All these things happened because He takes up the title of the Son of Man, and came and took on human flesh.[14] Not for Him, but for us. We are men, and so it had to be. Now this reconciliation would not be universal to all mankind, but a certain body of men would be redeemed and reconciled. This is the church, the body of Christ.

Colossians 1:13-14

"He has delivered us from the power of darkness and translated us into the kingdom of the Son of His love, in whom we have redemption through His blood, the forgiveness of sins."

Colossians 1:18

"And He is the head of the body, the church, who is the beginning, the firstborn from the dead, that in all things He may have the preeminence."

In all things Jesus Christ has the preeminence, the first place, and headship. As we have seen He is the head of all creation as the Creator. Here we see He is the Head of the body because the Son of Man is the firstborn from the dead. His death and shed blood is the means of the redemption of the believer/church (Col. 1:14). He goes into the glory first, as the forerunner, so that His body, the church, will follow. He goes into the Presence as the glorified Man, providing the means by which other men, His brethren, will go with Him later.

The Sons of God are the Heirs of the Father

The inheritance is now associated with this Man, for He has reconciled all things in the heavens and earth, things visible and invisible, back to God through His blood (Col. 1:20). But if we look closely we should be able to see that the inheritance is not given in this manner. It is not an inheritance given from God to man – in principle this doesn't make any sense. Rather, it is an inheritance given from Father to Son. The inheritance is a family thing. The Father will give it to the Son, who is appointed by Him as heir of all things (Heb. 1:2).

The believer is an heir of God and fellow heir with Christ (Rom. 8:17, Gal. 4:7). But how is this? It is not because we are now redeemed men, having our sins forgiven, and finally at peace with God (Col. 1:14, Rom. 5:1). This is a blessed first truth concerning our justification, but it does not explain why we are heirs. Also the church will eventually enter into the Presence behind the veil because the glorified Man has gone there already – by this, man will not fall short of the glory of God (Heb. 6:19-20, Rom. 3:23). Again, this is blessed truth, but it does not fully explain the inheritance of the saints. How is it that we are heirs?

Romans 8:16-17

"The Spirit Himself bears witness with our spirit that we are children of God, and if children, then heirs—heirs of God and joint heirs with Christ, if indeed we suffer with Him, that we may also be glorified together."

Galatians 4:6-7

"And because you are sons, God has sent forth the Spirit of His Son into your hearts, crying out, "Abba, Father!" Therefore you are no longer a slave but a son, and if a son, then an heir of God through Christ."

Galatians 3:26

"For you are all sons of God through faith in Christ Jesus."

We are heirs because we are now children. Previously we were not children, certainly not children of God. All we could scripturally say about our previous position is that we were by nature children of the first Adam, and by consequence of his disobedience, children of the devil (John 8:34-44). By nature, we were children of wrath and sons of disobedience (Eph. 2:1-3).

But now we are heirs of God because we are children of God. And it should benefit all believers if we could trace the development of these thoughts from the truths and realities of our redemption in Christ. How is it that the believer is now a child of God? Is it because your sins have been forgiven? This is not the reason. As a believer, Christ bore your sins on the tree and now they are gone. Guilt is associated with sins and so, for the believer all guilt should be gone. The believer now has peace with God (Rom. 5:1). This is your justification. But if the forgiveness of sins is all there is to your redemption, then God has left you in your original position – in Adam and in the flesh, and still with no potential to please God (Rom. 8:8-9).[15]

The Believer's new position – in Christ, the Second Adam

God hasn't just forgiven our sins and justified us. He did not leave us as the old man in Adam. God has done far more than this. He has changed our state, our position. By redemption we are no longer in the first Adam, but now in Christ, the second Adam. We are born of God.

John 1:12-13

"But as many as received Him, to them He gave the right to become children of God, to those who believe in His name: who were born, not of blood, nor of the will of the flesh, nor of the will of man, but of God."

Most of this verse is a contrast with being born in the first Adam – born of blood, of the will of the flesh, and of the will of man. However, the believer is now on the other side of the contrast and quite the opposite. We are born of God. By this birth we are children of God. By the Holy Spirit sent down to the earth, the Father is gathering a family, the body of Christ. The Father's family is centered in and around His Son, Jesus Christ. Through faith in Jesus Christ we are all sons of God (Gal. 3:26).

Death ended the Believer's relationship with the First Adam

We were crucified with Christ, knowing this, that our old man was crucified with Him (Gal. 2:20, Rom. 6:6). This is the death of your life in the first Adam. As a believer you died with Christ (Rom. 6:8). Your position and relationship to the first Adam was put to an end. But if we died with Christ, then we were also raised with Him (Col. 3:1, Rom. 6:4, 6:8, Eph. 2:5).

Romans 6:5

"For if we have been united together in the likeness of His death, certainly we also shall be in the likeness of His resurrection..."

The New Creation of the Second Adam

This is the new creation of God that we are in Jesus Christ (Gal. 6:15, II Cor. 5:17). This is the new position of the believer. It is the resurrection life of Christ (Col. 2:12). It is out of Adam and into the second Adam. It is the believer 'in Christ.' And it is the new creation of God because it is born of God. By this we are the children of God as sons. And we know, *"...if a son, then an heir of God through Christ."* (Gal. 4:7)

And because we are now sons, God has sent forth the Spirit of His Son into our hearts, crying out, "Abba, Father!" The Father places in the believer His seal of authenticity, the seal of the Spirit (Eph. 1:13). He is given the Spirit of adoption, the Spirit of sonship (Rom. 8:15, Gal. 4:6). The relationship established is the Father with the sons of God. We are born of God as children. "...and if children, then heirs – heirs of God and joint heirs with Christ." (Rom. 8:17)

The Father's children receive the Inheritance

Colossians 1:12

"...giving thanks to the Father who has qualified us to be partakers of the inheritance of the saints in the light."

It is the Father who gives the inheritance. It is the Son who is the appointed heir of all things. But we are now fellow heirs with the Son. We not only share in the glory of the Son of Man glorified (John 17:22), but we are the brethren of the Son (John 17:22), and equal heirs with Him in all He inherits (Of course He does not inherit His divinity or divine attributes. We do not share in this, except that the new creation is a partaking of the divine nature in relationship with God – II Pet. 1:4). The same inheritance Christ will be given is the one we will share in. It is an inheritance of all things created. It is the inheritance of the saints.

We are in Christ and He in us (John 14:20). The only life we have is the resurrected Christ living in us. As many of us as were baptized into Christ have put on Christ (Gal. 3:27). The body of Christ is the fullness of Him (Eph. 1:23). All the members of that one body, being many, are one body – so also is Christ (I Cor. 12:12). Both He who sanctifies and those who are being sanctified are all of one, for which reason He is not ashamed to call them brethren (Heb. 2:11). Those who are joined to the Lord are one Spirit with Him (I Cor.6:17).

The Rapture gathers the children of God for the Inheritance

The Son of Man has been exalted into the glory of God and sits at the right hand of God. But as we've previously taught, none of these events were for Him personally, but all for us. There will be given by the Father the inheritance of the saints. It is given to Christ and those in union with Him, His fellow brethren and heirs. *But the Father will not give this inheritance until all the heirs are present. All the sons will have to be there.*

And so, it is the rapture of the church that is the Lord gathering His brethren and returning to the Father. It is the entire body being taken from this earth. It is not a progression of individual deaths of believers from the day of Pentecost on. It is in a moment, in the twinkling of an eye. And it is all by the sovereign power of God, this resurrection and change. The Father will have His sons with Him. He will unite the body to the Head. It is not in the counsels of God for the Father to give an inheritance to a bodiless Head. The inheritance of all things must wait until all the sons are glorified. Jesus assured us that He will come for us all. And His coming is not the death of believers, but rather their resurrection and life. This is the blessed hope of the church.

Chapter 5: Endnotes

[12] Adam and Eve, before their fall in sin, are a remarkable type of Christ and the church. Adam is put to sleep and Eve is formed from out of him and then presented to him after he wakens. In fulfillment of this type, after the death of the second Adam, He awakes in resurrection and glory to have His bride presented to Him in glory. The church is formed out of Him. It is a church in glory and not on the earth. How else will it be a glorious church, not having spot or wrinkle or any such thing, holy without blemish? This can only come to pass for the church by the sovereign power of God. For the church to be presented in glory, and to be holy and without blemish, it can only be the sovereign work of God (Eph. 5:27). And this type teaches more. Everything Adam says after the presentation of Eve, and what God says concerning this relationship and marriage has a greater reality and substance in Christ and the church. For Christ and the church, the two will be one, and this will be eternally. Here we haven't even touched on the dominion given to Adam, and Eve as his help-meet. As I said, it is a most remarkable type and full of spiritual instruction (Eph. 5:32).

[13] Jesus Christ, being in the form of God and equal to God, took on human flesh. Only God could have done this. It was a change of state. All of the creation of God was confined to its present state, and for all of it there was no possibility of change. All of creation became defiled and corrupted by the disobedience of Adam – the creation was subjected to futility, not willingly, but in hope (Rom. 8:20). But this change of state for the second person of the Godhead only God could do, and it was necessary, even in a sense demanded. Without it all would be universally lost concerning the destiny of man.

Jesus Christ took on flesh. His change of state we often call His humiliation; by it He lowered Himself below the angels for a time. Truly He did this for the sole reason of suffering death and completing a redemptive work by that death. The believer was crucified with Christ. Our previous state in Adam is done with by this death. We are now a new creation in Christ. This is our new state. It is in the second Adam. It is born of God. It is a son of God. It is a new state and a new position. But it was all God's work. Only God could have done this.

[14] The Scriptures tell us, "For indeed He does not give aid to angels, but He does give aid to the seed of Abraham. Therefore, in all things He had to be made like His brethren..." God takes up the cause of man. He does not

redeem angels. This adds further to our understanding of the necessity of the work of the Son of Man and that presently there is a Man in glory, sitting at the right hand of God. He had to be made like His brethren – not universal redemption of mankind, but that of His brethren.

[15] Unfortunately, many Christians continue to live in guilt, not believing that all their sins are forgiven or can be forgiven. They do not have peace with God, nor do they have any true sense of security in their salvation. Their eternal life is not so eternal, and they live under the fear of possible judgment from God. This is a sad condition, and at the root of this type of unscriptural faith is the Arminian leaven. They must do certain things to secure the eternalness of their salvation, as well as avoiding other things. Jesus isn't the Captain of their salvation, but rather they are, and they are responsible for maintaining it. It is not as Jesus said, *"And I give them eternal life, and they shall never perish; neither shall anyone snatch them out of My hand. My Father, who has given them to Me, is greater than all; and no one is able to snatch them out of My Father's hand."* (John 10:28-29, 6:37-40, 17:11-12) It is not an understanding that God sees fit to keep His sovereign work, but instead, man being responsible for keeping himself. When the scriptures ask, "Who shall separate us from the love of Christ?" they quickly add that they themselves can, if certain things happen. "If God is for us, who can be against us?" Well, they say, you are the only one who can be, and you will lose your salvation if you aren't careful to do things right.

This type of thinking never gives peace and will never bring one to peace with God. It is always a fearful looking for judgment and for the appointed day of their death. But this is the portion of all unbelievers (Heb. 9:27). For the believer, Christ has put away sin by the sacrifice of Himself (Heb. 9:26) and was offered once to bear the sins of many (Heb. 9:28) – so then, we are those who eagerly wait for Him to appear for us a second time, apart from sin and judgment, for the end of our salvation, the glorifying of our bodies. Obviously, His first coming was on account of sin and to bear the sins of many. It was for God to judge sin in the flesh and to righteously deal with sins (Heb. 9:26, 28). He will come again for those who eagerly wait for Him. This second time He does not come for the judgment of sin or to bear sins, but clearly apart from sin and for salvation – for those eagerly waiting (the believer/church). This second appearing is so different in character from the first, which was for the judgment of sin for them. The second appearing is for sin to be removed from their flesh by the glorifying of their bodies. He will come again for the consummation of their salvation. There is therefore now no condemnation to those who are in Christ Jesus (Rom. 8:1).

Notes

Chapter 6:

The Shadows of the Rapture

The Spirit of God's use of types and shadows as pictures prefiguring future events is quite extensive in Scripture. By them the believer receives instruction concerning greater truths and realities that are the fulfillment of the types. The fulfillment is always the substance of greater value. The type is always the shadow cast by the true substance and always prefigures the substance.

The teaching by the Spirit through God's use of types and shadows in His Word is for the believer/church. It is not for Israel. They do not have the Spirit of God, therefore cannot know the things of God (I Cor. 2:11). Not only do they not have the Spirit of truth, but they cannot receive Him, being very much part of the world.

The Believer's privileged position

John 14:17

"...the Spirit of truth, whom the world cannot receive, because it neither sees Him nor knows Him; but you know Him, for He dwells with you and will be in you."

The believer has the Spirit of truth in him. This is a significant difference between the believer/church and Israel. The believer has been placed in an entirely new position from that of the first Adam. We are the new creation of God in Christ. And in this position as sons of God we have been given certain privileges. One important benefit of this new position is that we are no longer called servants but friends, so that we may fully know all that the master is doing (John 15:15). This particular privilege is about the imparting of spiritual knowledge concerning the plan and counsels of God. It is only for the believer because we have been given and sealed with the Spirit of truth.

It is the Spirit who searches all things, yes, the deep things of God (I Cor. 2:10) – and so God has revealed these things to us through His Spirit. By the Spirit we might know all the things that have been freely given to us by God. We have the mind of Christ (I Cor. 2:12, 16). Now this privilege is characterized for us in the Old Testament type of Abraham. He was a friend of God. And as a friend it was revealed to him what God was about to do in His judgment of Sodom and Gomorrah (Gen 18:17). In this character Abraham becomes a type and shadow of the privileged position of the believer as the friend of God. The believer can know the things of God, the plan of God, even those things that God will do that do not directly concern us, as it was with Abraham.

Types and Shadows as teaching examples

1 Corinthians 10:1-11

(1) "Moreover, brethren, I do not want you to be unaware that all our fathers were under the cloud, all passed through the sea, (2) all were baptized into Moses in the cloud and in the sea, (3) all ate the same spiritual food, (4) and all drank the same spiritual drink. For they drank of that spiritual Rock that followed them, and that Rock was Christ. (5) But with most of them God was not well pleased, for their bodies were scattered in the wilderness."

(6) "Now these things became our examples, to the intent that we should not lust after evil things as they also lusted. (7) And

do not become idolaters as were some of them. As it is written, "The people sat down to eat and drink, and rose up to play." (8) Nor let us commit sexual immorality, as some of them did, and in one day twenty-three thousand fell; (9) nor let us tempt Christ, as some of them also tempted, and were destroyed by serpents; (10) nor complain, as some of them also complained, and were destroyed by the destroyer. (11) Now all these things happened to them as examples, and they were written for our admonition, upon whom the ends of the ages have come."

All of the events from the Old Testament and Israel are instructional examples for the believer. However, many of these events and things are types and shadows. *All types and shadows are instructional examples, but all examples are not types and shadows.* For example in the passage above, there are instructional examples that teach directly and literally.

1. The believer should not lust after evil things (v.6)

2. The believer should not become an idolater. Israel immediately made a golden calf when waiting on God and Moses at the foot of Mt. Sinai (v. 7)

3. The believer should not commit sexual immorality. Israel's judgment from God in this incidence was 23,000 dying in one day (v.8)

4. The believer should not tempt Christ. By this many in Israel died by serpent bites (v.9)

5. The believer should not murmur and complain against God. Many Israelites died at the hand of the destroyer (v.10)

All these things happened with Israel when they were in the wilderness and they are examples that teach the believer direct truths and godly morals. It remains however in a general sense, that Israel in the wilderness is a type of our present walk as believers on this earth and in this world. Also it is true that Israel, viewed corporately as a people in the wilderness, is a type of professing Christianity in the world.

Israel as a corporate People or Nation

If we trace the use of this type – Israel as a people and nation – it becomes instructional concerning redemptive realities today. In the first five verses of the above passage Israel is viewed corporately as a people.

1.) All the fathers were under the cloud, all passed through the sea (v. 1)

2.) All were baptized into Moses, in the cloud/sea (v. 2)

3.) All ate the same spiritual food (v. 3). The manna that Israel ate is a type of Christ, the true bread of life given by God from above (John 6:32-35, 41, 48-51, 58)

4.) All drank the same spiritual drink (v. 4). The Rock is also a type of Christ and the water from it a type of eternal life (John 4:13-14)

The point of emphasis is Israel being viewed as a people, as a corporate entity. But God was not pleased with this people. As a nation Israel was a mixture of faith and unbelief. This mixture leads directly to their experiences in the wilderness, the judgment of certain ones, and many bodies being scattered there (v.5).

Hebrews 3:16-19

(16) For who, having heard, rebelled? Indeed, was it not all who came out of Egypt, led by Moses? (17) Now with whom was He angry forty years? Was it not with those who sinned, whose corpses fell in the wilderness? (18) And to whom did He swear that they would not enter His rest, but to those who did not obey? (19) So we see that they could not enter in because of unbelief.

In this passage Israel is viewed as a people when it says, "*...was it not all who came out of Egypt, led by Moses?*" The whole nation came out. But all of them didn't go into the land. Jehovah was angry with many of them for the span of forty years. He swore that many of them would not enter into the land. Many corpses fell in judgment in the wilderness.

The mixture of Professing Christianity

Christianity on the earth and in this world (the wilderness) has always been a mixture of wheat and tares in a crop planted in the field of this world. The wheat was sown by the Son of Man, the tares by the wicked one. They exist together, mixed together, until the harvest time in the end (Matt. 13:24-30, 37-43). What is clear is that just like with Israel, there is a mixture of faith and unbelief in professing Christianity.

If we trace the experiences of Israel, from their slavery as a nation in Egypt to their entrance into the Promised Land under Joshua, we may readily see how Israel is a type prefiguring greater realities to come. To do this we will look at a list of the different types that are seen.

Israel in types and shadows

- The Passover lamb Israel ate and the blood of this lamb on the doorposts staid the hand of God's righteous judgment of Israel, while the firstborns of Egypt suffered. Christ is the believer's Passover lamb (I Cor. 5:7).

- Egypt is a type of the world, Pharaoh a type of Satan, the god of this world. Israel was in slavery to the world (Egypt) and its god. Israel needed deliverance and separation from Egypt and its Pharaoh. God, in sovereign power and glory accomplishes this deliverance and salvation (Rom. 9:17). For the believer in Christ, this type is fulfilled in true redemption, a separation from this world and its god, by the power of God (Eph. 2:1-5). For Israel it is only an external redemption and deliverance. It is types and shadows, and in the flesh only.

- Israel's passage through the Red Sea is type of faith in the blood of Christ in redemption and salvation for the believer. Moses stretched out his hands and said, "Behold the salvation of the Lord." Passing on dry ground is type of the sovereign power of God in the work of salvation – we are His workmanship in Christ Jesus.

- Both the manna they ate and the rock that gave them water are types of Christ, and how He gives eternal life (John 4:10, 14, and 6:48-51). What they ate and drank from God only sustained them for one day. It was not the substance that is Christ, but only a shadow prefiguring Him. However, this does readily point out how Judaism is a walk by sight – water coming out of a rock and food dropping from the sky. The Jews demand a sign and are led by signs. In the wilderness Israel would lift up their heads and look with their eyes to see where the cloud by day or the pillar of fire by night would lead them on their walk.

- The law given to Israel at Mt. Sinai is Judaism. It is a walk by sight and a religion of the flesh. It is God's one true religion given to man in Adam, for the purpose of separating Israel on the earth from all the other man-made religions and human idolatry. In this sense Judaism is God's religion for the earth and the earthly calling. This will become abundantly clear during the coming millennium. Then Israel will be exalted as the greatest nation on the face of the earth, and become the center of the government of God (Ex. 19:5, Deut. 28:1-14, Deut. 32:8).

- In the wilderness Israel wandered for forty years as a mixed people of faith and unbelief. This is a type of the spoiled crop of wheat and tares in professing Christianity in the world. Israel wanders in the wilderness and never sets up residence in it. The believer also is on a walk on this earth and in this world, always a pilgrim traveling. Where we are headed to is the rest of God, just as Israel was headed to the land.

- The Promised Land is a type of the rest (Sabbath) of God for the believer/church in glory. In the type, God swore that many would not enter His rest because of their unbelief (Heb. 3:17-19). They would not enter the land, but their corpses fell in the wilderness. The reality of the Promised Land is for Israel saved as a remnant in the end. Israel is the earthly calling of God. For the believer/church, we enter into the rest of God, the glory of God, where we have ceased from our works as God did from His (Heb. 4:10).

- Israel crossing over the Jordan into the land is type of the believer/church entering into the glory of God through its rapture from the earth and this world (wilderness). Joshua leads Israel from the wilderness into the land, just as Jesus catches up the church from the earth and world to bring it to glory (John 14:3, and I Thess. 4:16-17). Joshua is a type of Christ. Upon entrance into the land, Israel is immediately circumcised (Josh. 5:6-7). This is a type that depicts sin being removed from the believer's flesh and our bodies glorified. Israel crossing on dry ground is the display of the exceeding greatness of God's power towards us who believe (Eph. 1:19) in the rapture of the church and entrance into His glory. This is the blessed hope of the church.

Israel's wanderings in the Wilderness – the Believer's walk in this World

The believer's walk in this world is reflected in a general way in type by the fact that Israel wandered in the wilderness. The believer's walk is in the world, but not of the world. Previous to Israel's wilderness experience they were delivered out of slavery in Egypt under Pharaoh. Israel was part of Egypt (the world) and then they were delivered apart from Egypt (the world). This type is the previous state of the believer – part of the world, a slave to sin, and under the prince of the power of the air (Eph. 2:2-3, John 8:34). Israel in Egypt is type of the believer's previous state before redemption and deliverance. We all walked according to the course of this world. Yet it was the Father and the Son who chose us out of the world (John 15:19). Now in Christ, we are not part of the world as Christ is not part of the world (John 17:14).

The wilderness is also a type of the world. However Israel wandering in the wilderness is different from Israel in bondage in Egypt. In Egypt they are a type of the unbeliever before salvation, as part of the world. In the wilderness they are a type of the believer now saved and not of the world, but left behind in this world as a stranger and pilgrim (John 17:11). The believer is on a walk in the wilderness (world).

The Rapture – the Church entering into God's Rest

Israel was always headed for the Promised Land, at least early on in their wilderness experience. The believer/church walking in this world has a destination as well – the rest and glory of God. Israel crossing the Jordan to their destination, the land, is the church being taken to their destination – into the glory of God. The promise remains of entering His rest (Heb. 4:1) and we who have believed do enter that rest (Heb. 4:3). Joshua did not give Israel rest, even though he led them into the land (Heb. 4:8).[16] There remains therefore a rest for the people of God – His rest, God's rest, God's glory (Heb. 4:9). The rapture of the church will take the believer into His rest.

Noah and the Jewish Remnant

There is another shadow found in the scriptures of the rapture of the church. We are all aware of Noah and his family preserved in the midst of judgment. They were protected from harm in the ark with the animals when God destroyed the world that proceeded from Adam. The sin of man filled the earth and it grieved the heart of God (Gen. 6:5-7). Noah and his family were saved through judgment.[17] As a type they do not represent the church, but rather the Jewish remnant preserved through the hour of trial that is to come upon the whole world (Rev. 3:10).

Enoch and the Rapture of the Church

Genesis 5:21-24

(21) Enoch lived sixty-five years, and begot Methuselah. (22) After he begot Methuselah, Enoch walked with God three hundred

years, and had sons and daughters. (23) So all the days of Enoch were three hundred and sixty-five years. (24) And Enoch walked with God; and he was not, for God took him.

Enoch is a type of the church. He walked with God. The true church walks on this earth as sons of God and with Him. God took Enoch before the judgment in the time of Noah. God will remove the church before the time of His coming judgment of this world. And there is more to the story of Enoch.

Jude 1:14-15

"Now Enoch, the seventh from Adam, prophesied about these men also, saying, "Behold, the Lord comes with ten thousands of His saints, (15) to execute judgment on all, to convict all who are ungodly among them of all their ungodly deeds which they have committed in an ungodly way, and of all the harsh things which ungodly sinners have spoken against Him."

It was revealed to Enoch about the coming judgment and God used Him to prophesy about it. But this prophecy is really about a judgment of this present world; this judgment he speaks of is yet to come. The church also has been made aware of the coming judgment of the world. We have been given the Old Testament scriptures containing the writings of the prophets as well as the book of Revelation. The church stands in this privileged position like Enoch. But as Enoch was taken before the judgment, so will we be taken. This is the believer's earnest expectation. This is the blessed hope of the church.

Chapter 6: Endnotes

[16] Joshua led Israel into the land, but this was not rest for Israel – Hebrews 4:8. This becomes an important understanding in viewing Israel as a type and shadow of the future church. Once Israel crosses the Jordan and they are in the land, and are circumcised, all the types and shadows end as far as the church. The Promised Land is a type of the rest and glory of God for the believer/church. The end of Israel being a type prefiguring the church is this (Heb. 4:10) – *"For he who has entered His rest has himself also ceased from his works as God did from His."* When the believer enters the rest and glory of God there will be no battles to be fought, no enemies to be driven out. We cease from our works. After the rapture of the church, its removal from the earth, and entrance into the presence of God, three spiritual truths become a physical reality for the believer.

1. Sin from Adam is removed from the flesh for our bodies to be glorified. Much of our present struggle as a believer is against the flesh. One purpose of the presence of the Holy Spirit within us is the spiritual energy He supplies to us for this struggle – for the flesh lusts against the Spirit, and the Spirit against the flesh (Gal. 5:17). However in glory there is no sin and there is no temptation. We have been conformed into the image of His Son by sin removed from the flesh and our bodies glorified.

2. The church will have physically departed the earth and world. Presently, as believers, we are on a walk in the wilderness. As we walk in this world our feet get dirty. We have a faithful High Priest who is constantly washing the feet of the believer. This world is defilement for the believer in his walk in it. But this will all change after the rapture, having been physically removed from this world.

3. After the rapture of the church, Satan will no longer be a source of temptations, tribulations, or attacks for the body of Christ. Presently he is the god and prince of the world that the believer walks in as a stranger. By the armor of God we quench all the fiery darts of the wicked one (Eph. 6:12-18). Resist the devil and he will flee from the believer. He is a defeated devil presently (John 12:31, Heb. 2:14-15). It is just

that the time of his final physical judgments has not come. These physical judgments will be in this manner and order:

a.) He will be physically removed from the heavens and cast down to the earth (Rev. 12:7-12). He comes down with great wrath, knowing his time is short.

b.) He will be chained and cast into the bottomless pit for the duration of the millennium (Rev. 20:1-3).

c.) After his last temptation of the nations at the end of the millennium, he is cast into the lake of fire eternally (Rev. 20:10).

It remains then, that the types and shadows prefiguring the church stop when Israel enters the land under Joshua and he circumcises them. Israel in the land is a nation under the law and being tested by God for obedience. In the land Israel fails in responsibility after the battle of Jericho. Then they write a history of failure in responsibility from that point on, with occasional bright points in King David and the early years of Solomon. There is no similitude in this to the church now in the rest of God.

What the battle of Jericho and the events surrounding it prefigure is how Jehovah will display His awesome sovereign power on behalf of the Jewish remnant in the end under the oppression of the Antichrist and the Roman beast. This is a type prefiguring the saving of the nation of Israel in the end. It will be a time of the return of the glory of Jehovah in the midst of Israel for the defeat of their enemies. This glory hasn't been in Israel since the time of Ezekiel. The sovereign power of God, the glory of Jehovah, and the Ark of the Covenant play the dominant role in the battle of Jericho. Israel does nothing but walk and shout. This prefigures how the sovereign power of God will deliver Israel in the end. Jesus, their Messiah, will either destroy or drive out their enemies from the land. But as a type it has nothing to do with the church, which is in the rest and glory of God and has ceased from its works as God has from His.

Other types that point to Israel in the end (and not to the church) are found in Israel's experiences in the Promised Land. David is the suffering king which points to Jesus Christ having suffered for the nation (John 11:50-51). David also is the victorious king who defeated all the enemies of Israel. Jesus Christ, in His return, will do the same for the nation, only on a much grander and glorious scale. Solomon, the son of David, is a type of the true Son of David. Solomon sat on the throne of Jehovah in Jerusalem, built an earthly house for Jehovah, and reigned in righteousness and peace. These types point to the reign of the Son of Man from earthly Jerusalem during the millennium, the true Son of David as Israel's Messianic Prince, and the royal priesthood of Melchizedek (Christ) – righteousness and peace and blessing to Israel after the defeat of their enemies. But all these things are types that point to Israel in the end, not to the church. Again, Israel being a type prefiguring the church stops after Israel enters the land and is circumcised under Joshua. In this Joshua is a type of Christ who in the rapture will lead the church into God's rest and glory (I Thess. 4:16-17).

[17] There is a Biblical principle established in God's dealings with Israel as the earthly calling. Noah and those with him, representing the future Jewish remnant in type, are saved and preserved through judgment. In principle, Israel is always delivered through judgment. Noah has this character in his experience representing them. Israel, as a nation, was delivered out of Egypt with and through the judgments of God. In the end, the sealed Jewish remnant is the woman on the earth in Revelation 12, who flees into the wilderness, where she has a place prepared by God (Rev. 12:6) for three and a half years. Being sealed, she will be preserved and protected during the time of great tribulation on the earth. This time is known as Jacob's trouble (Jer. 30:7). "But he shall be saved out of it."

There is another type that relates to this Biblical principle in Israel, and is seen in the different positions between Abraham and Lot concerning the judgment of Sodom and Gomorrah. Lot is a type of the end-time Jewish remnant that is delivered through judgment. Abraham however is type of the church, viewing the judgment of these cities from a high and distant place.

Abraham is the Old Testament character who has the greatest connection of any to the church. This is seen in the types and shadows in his character and experiences that prefigure the church.

- Abraham's calling is like the church/believer – it was a calling out from his present world. God said to him, "Get out of your country, from your kindred and from your father's house..." (Gen. 12:1) God wanted Abraham separated from the present world. The believer's/church's calling is heavenly (Heb. 3:1). While in this world we are not of it. By the rapture we are physically removed from it to the heavens.

- Abraham walked in the land as a stranger and pilgrim (Heb. 11:13). It was a walk by faith – "By faith he sojourned in the land of promise as in a foreign country...for he waited for a city which has foundations, whose builder and maker is God." In this, Abraham's faith was the substance of the things he hoped for, the evidence of the things he did not see (Heb. 11:1). In all this, the believer is practically the same.

- The other character of Abraham's faith was that he believed in the God who raises the dead (Rom. 4:17, Heb. 11:19). The believer is similar to the father of the faithful:

Romans 4:23-25

Now it was not written for his sake alone that it was imputed to him, but also for us. It shall be imputed to us who believe in Him who raised up Jesus our Lord from the dead, who was delivered up because of our offenses, and was raised because of our justification.

We believe in the God who raised Jesus from the dead (Rom 10:9). But more than this, the believer knows that at the rapture God will resurrect the church by His exceedingly great power that was prefigured in raising Christ from the dead.

- Abraham was a friend of God. The believer is not a servant but a friend of God. We are privileged to know the things God will do just as Abraham.

- Abraham watched the judgment of Sodom from a remote and high place. After the rapture, the church will view the judgment of the world from a high and distant place.

- Abraham's greatest connection to the church is his connection to his one Seed, who is Christ, and in that the covenant of promise was confirmed in Christ. This plays out in his only-begotten son Isaac, who is type of Jesus Christ in resurrection (Heb. 11:17-19). The church can only be seen as hidden 'in Christ,' the one true Seed of Abraham.

Notes

Chapter 7:
The Church World Long Asleep

The Biblical principle of responsibility in man runs through Scripture from beginning to end, to one degree or another. This principle has a distinct history that can be traced. At different periods of time since the creation of the world God has dealt differently with this principle. All His dealings with the principle serve to bring out, in a progressive way, the enhancement and exaltation of His glory. In the final state of creation – the new heavens and the new earth of the eternal state – God will be all in all in the divine glory (I Cor. 15:28). This is where everything in the counsels of God is headed, and there is no stopping it. In view of this, we should be able to see God's ways in dealing with this principle in man, and that it will be for the glory of God.

From the time man was created and placed in paradise to the sending of Messiah to Israel, God used this principle of responsibility as a means of testing man. When God is testing He gives a command or laws. He is looking for obedience. This is the fruit God is seeking to find in man. During this period of time God's testing has only found failure in man. *The history of man in the scriptures proves his failures, and this becomes the testimony of God concerning man. Failure is always the outcome in the testing of responsibility, and this usually immediately.*

God's first testing

To fully understand both the principle and the testing, we must look deeper at this period of time. Man was created and placed in the garden. His state and condition was one of innocence – he had no knowledge whatsoever of good and evil. In this state he would not even be able to define these words. He was given one command with consequences, and obedience was expected by God his Creator. This was the responsibility given to Adam and this is how it was tested.

Adam believed and trusted the words of the serpent rather than the words of God. He was convinced by Satan that God was holding a blessing back from him. He did this in the exercise of his 'free will.'[18] His disobedience brought the consequences of judgment not just to himself, but onto the entire human race (he being its federal head). All mankind now had 'sin' passed on to them, and all men became sinners from this point forward (Rom. 5:12). There was failure by man from the very beginning when given responsibility. Man would never be the same as he was created by God at first. He could never return to innocence. What he became was quite different from what he was in the garden before his fall.

God testing responsibility by the Law

The next specific testing of man is the giving of the law to Israel at Mt. Sinai. With this we must have certain understandings of the differences involved in this particular testing. The law contained commandments from God that would test responsibility, and He was still looking for obedience as a fruit. The principle of responsibility is the same, and the testing is basically the same; but this time man is fallen and a sinner. *Does this make a difference?* The full understanding of the state of man before the fall compared to after the fall is of the greatest importance. Before, he was innocent and without the knowledge of good and evil. After? Well, let's just allow the Scriptures to speak to this.

Mankind in Adam – Fallen Man and Utter Depravity

1. Man was now a sinner, and this is true of all descendants of Adam (Rom. 5:8, 12, 19). All men were dead in trespasses and sins (Eph. 2:1). In Adam, all are sinners.

2. Man was fallen and lost (Matt. 18:11, Luke 19:10). In Adam, all are lost.

3. All men walked according to the course of this world. All men walked according to the prince of the air. All men were sons of disobedience (Eph. 2:2). In Adam, all men are of the world and disobedient to God.

4. All men were by birth and nature, children of wrath (Eph. 2:3). In Adam, by natural birth, all men are destined for condemnation and wrath (Rom. 5:16, 18).

5. All men are in the flesh, and have no ability or chance to please God (Rom. 8:8). In Adam means the unbeliever is in the flesh.

6. All men are guilty before God (Rom. 3:19). All men fall short (Rom. 3:23). In Adam, man cannot have a relationship with God, or any hope of ever entering His presence and glory.

7. All men are without strength to change their state (Rom. 5:6). In Adam, man has no resource to cause a change, no power to change, and most important to realize, no will to change.

8. All men were enemies of God (Rom. 5:10, 8:7). In Adam, the carnal mind is nothing but enmity against God.

9. There are none righteous among men, no, not one (Rom. 3:10). In Adam, all man's righteousness is but filthy rags (Is. 64:6)

10. There are none among men who seek after God (Rom. 3:11). In Adam, all men go their own way (Is. 53:6) and seek to do their own will (Dan. 11:36, John 6:38).

11. All men are now slaves to sin (John 8:34, Rom. 5:21). All men now possess a conscience, but it is defiled and corrupted in sin. In Adam, all men's wills are a slave to sin and under its reign in the flesh.

When man was chased out of paradise, this was his condition – one of utter depravity. He was lost, having no hope and without God in the world (Eph. 2:12). So when man was tested in responsibility this second time by giving him the law at Mt. Sinai, what do you think was going to happen? The law was given to sinners. They failed immediately.

Israel is the Test Case for man in Adam

This doesn't even address another important issue that comes up with the giving of the law at Mt. Sinai. And this is a question that must be adequately answered. Why was the law only given to Israel? How can we possibly think that the law was for all mankind when God Himself only gave it to the Jews? We can't. It wasn't for all mankind. It was for the testing of responsibility, and Israel alone was the test case. When the test case failed it proved God's point. God had no need of testing the Gentiles. Israel, as specifically chosen by God and privileged by God above all nations, had failed as the test case. Therefore, as proven, all mankind was guilty before God (Rom. 3:19).

The giving of the law proved the utter depravity of all mankind. Sin was passed on from Adam and had accomplished a comprehensive work in the entire human race. Truly the judgment which came from one offence resulted in condemnation of all men (Rom. 5:12, 16). The entrance of the law simply made the proof of this more obvious (Rom. 5:20). God wasn't convincing Himself, He wanted to show and convince man.[19]

The Final Testing

The last testing of this principle of responsibility was when God sent His Son into the world (Matt. 21:37). This was the last time God would test man in Adam, looking for fruit.[20] He came unto His own as their Messiah, but His own did not receive Him (John 1:10-11). In this last testing by God, He found nothing but failure. Israel would not have the Son but delivered Him over to the Gentiles. God was looking for fruit, but only found leaves adorning the fig tree (Matt. 21:19).[21] By this, God condemned the entire world at that time.

The history of man was complete – the world was judged (John 12:31). The result of man's responsibility was fully brought out. When man was without the law he produced intolerable sin (Rom. 1, 2). When under the law he produced transgression. The prophets were sent to call him back to the law but they abused and killed them. And when visited by grace and blessing, man simply refused grace by killing the Son (Matt. 21:33-40). All the testing of responsibility proved that man, driven out of Paradise, *naturally* produced sin. Man in Adam could not be subject to the law of God. Man in the flesh was proven to be an enemy of God (Rom. 8:7-8). God had shown divine love in patience, however only received hatred from man, and that without a cause (John 15:22-25). Such was sin and such was man.

The principle of responsibility does not cease to exist at this time. It's just that God's ways in dealing with it, from this point forward, change. He was finished with the testing of man in his own resources. Man in Adam was proven lost. Yet the principle had to be addressed, and done so by God in a just and holy manner. Man in Adam could only offer sin and failure, lawlessness and transgressions. As I said, the testing of the principle was complete. The results were in. Man is proven by God as utterly depraved.

Romans 3:23-26

(23) "for all have sinned and fall short of the glory of God, (24) being justified freely by His grace through the redemption that is in Christ Jesus, (25) whom God set forth as a propitiation by His blood, through faith, to demonstrate His righteousness, because in His forbearance God had passed over the sins that were previously committed, (26) to demonstrate at the present time His righteousness, that He might be just and the justifier of the one who has faith in Jesus."

God's dealing with Responsibility

God's ways in dealing with this principle would be through sovereign grace by the cross. He would freely justify through redemption in Christ. The believer's responsibility in the first Adam has been addressed. God has taken it up and done so according to His own holiness and righteousness. The short version of these redemptive truths is found in this: Christ bore our sins and was made to be sin for us, and God condemned Him on the cross. Christ received the believer's judgment and condemnation that was rightly ours in Adam. God was appeased and exonerated, the blood of Christ being the propitiation towards Him for man. The Son of Man had glorified God in all His work, and so He enters, as Man, into God's glory. God remains just and becomes the justifier of the one who has faith in Jesus.

The Believer's individual responsibility

Once we are settled and secure in our salvation, we must realize that there now exists two areas of responsibility before God. Individually we were drawn by the Father to faith in Jesus Christ (John 6:44), by which we each became a son of God (Gal. 3:26). We were placed in this relationship first, being sealed by the Spirit of sonship (Eph. 1:13). This is personal. It is individual faith and individual sonship resulting in being individually sealed by the Spirit. From this relationship – that of the Father with a son – flows our individual responsibility as believers. We are sons of the Father God and our responsibility is realized in our sonship.[22]

Professing Christianity's corporate responsibility

There is a second area of responsibility found in professing Christianity – that of the spoiled crop of wheat and tares in the field of the unbelieving world (Matt. 13:37-43). This crop has a candlestick that must shine to this dark and sinful world. The candlestick, and the brightness by which it shines, is the corporate responsibility of all of Christendom (Rev. 1:12-13). On the earth the responsibility of professing Christianity has been placed into the hands of men. The testimony of Scripture is that from the apostolic days of the church, the light from the candlestick has been progressively diminishing.

The Spoiled Crop in the Field

- <u>Professing Christianity</u> – all that profess the name of Jesus Christ. It is wheat and tares mixed together. The Son of Man planted the wheat, while the wicked one planted the tares (Matt. 13:37-39). The mixture remains undisturbed in the field of the world until the harvest at the end of the age.

- <u>Christianity</u> – all that adhere to some form of the Christian faith. When this term is used in its true meaning it references the body of Christ, the true church. *When the world uses this term* they are referencing all of professing Christianity, and usually the pope as its head, the Catholic Church as the main representative entity.

- <u>The Church World</u> – the great tree that grows up in the field of the world – Matt. 13:31-32. It becomes a great earthly power. This is similar to the meaning of the word 'Christendom.'

All three of the above terms with their definitions could be used interchangeably with the idea of the spoiled crop in the field. What is important to distinguish is that none of the terms define the true church – the body of Christ, the wheat planted by the Son of Man. The spoiled crop is all that professes Christ. It is certain that it contains the true church, but it is far more than this. On the earth and in the world (field), it is always wheat and tares mixed together, and it is ripening in evil to the end. It is the work of the Son of Man and the work of Satan mixed together in one corporate entity – professing Christianity.

Matthew 13:25

"...but while men slept, his enemy came and sowed tares among the wheat and went his way."

The words 'while men slept' describe the corporate responsibility of leaders and ministers in professing Christianity, allowing the enemy to come in and sow tares. This allows evil and corruption to fester and grow in the church world. And the Lord knows that man cannot be responsible for rectifying the situation, and so the mixture of professing Christianity remains as it is until the harvest time at the end (Matt. 13:28-30). This is what the kingdom of heaven has been like for nearly two thousand years.

Matthew 25:1-12

(1) "Then the kingdom of heaven shall be likened to ten virgins who took their lamps and went out to meet the bridegroom. (2) Now five of them were wise, and five were foolish. (3) Those who were foolish took their lamps and took no oil with them, (4) but the wise took oil in their vessels with their lamps. (5) But while the bridegroom was delayed, they all slumbered and slept."

(6) "And at midnight a cry was heard: 'Behold, the bridegroom is coming; go out to meet him!' (7) Then all those virgins arose and trimmed their lamps. (8) And the foolish said to the wise, 'Give us some of your oil, for our lamps are going out.' (9) But the wise answered, saying, 'No, lest there should not be enough for us and you; but go rather to those who sell, and buy for yourselves.' (10) And while they went to buy, the bridegroom came, and those who were ready went in with him to the wedding; and the door was shut."

(11) "Afterward the other virgins came also, saying, 'Lord, Lord, open to us!' (12) But he answered and said, 'Assuredly, I say to you, I do not know you.'"

Christendom Slumbering and Sleeping

This also is a parable concerning the kingdom of heaven. It is symbolic of certain features present today in the church world, one of which is a view of corporate responsibility spanning nearly two thousand years. Let's highlight some of the important features for our discussion.

- The ten virgins have the corporate composition of five wise and five foolish. This represents the mixture that exists in professing Christianity. The mixture is of the corporate entity, and that is the view we are given here, not individuals or individual responsibility.

- All the virgins look very similar to each other and therefore are difficult to tell apart. They all initially go out together, go back in to sleep together, and awake together to go back out. They all have the candlesticks of responsibility, regardless of whether they are foolish or wise.

- In the parable the one job or task of responsibility is distinct and clear – all were to remain awake and alert, looking and waiting for the bridegroom to return.

- The slumbering and sleeping (v. 5) is failure in responsibility by professing Christianity.

- At a certain time close to the bridegrooms' return, a midnight cry is sounded. All ten are awakened by the cry in order to go back out. The awakening serves to expose the true differences between the wise and the foolish.

Jesus is the bridegroom. Before the day of Pentecost He went away, and He is still away. He promised to return (John 14:2-3). When He does, it is for those who are His, those that He personally knows (v. 12). The foolish virgins were told that He does not know them.

The singular task of responsibility was to remain awake and alert for the coming of the bridegroom. This is what the parable is teaching. His coming for us is the rapture of the church. His coming for us should be a constant expectation of the believer, as it was to be for the entire group of virgins. The promise of His coming for us was to be comfort in the midst of a world that only offers us hatred and tribulation (John 14:1-2, 15:18-19, 16:33, 17:14). All of professing Christianity has failed in this task and has been sleeping for hundreds of years (v. 5). After the first century this doctrine essentially disappeared from the church world, along with many others. Ephesus had departed from its first position and would not return, signaling the beginning of the decay and decline of professing Christianity in the world (Rev. 2:1-5).

The Awakening of the Reformation

Like Pentecost, the early sixteenth century Reformation was a sovereign work of God. Two great truths that had been lost to the church world for some time came to light by the work of the Spirit.

1. The authority of Scripture as the only inspired Word of God and thus, for the Christian, the only proper guide to faith and practice. This is a biblical truth about the integrity of Scripture, declaring it as the only place from which we may find the truth of God (II Tim. 3:16 – 4:4). The church is not the authority of God on earth. Rather, it is the Scriptures.

2. Justification of the believer by faith. This is a scriptural truth out of the Word of God, obviously of great importance.

Both of these teachings had been lost for centuries from the time of the early church. During the reformation the Holy Spirit brings them to light, and they, in a sense, are rediscovered.[20]

The Midnight Cry

The parable of the virgins speaks of a midnight cry going out awakening the church world (v. 6). It is an awakening to the original task the virgins were given – the expectancy of the bridegroom coming and being alert and ready for this event. The rapture of the church is taught in Paul's epistles to the first century church. Then the teaching disappears for centuries. The midnight cry is the rediscovery of this particular doctrine and truth. It is an awakening to a teaching which has been long lost. Christ will come for His own and take them to where He is now (John 13:36, 14:3). The midnight cry was first sounded some 180 years ago in England in a movement known as the Brethren. This group brought back to the church world the doctrine of the rapture. Today His return for us is even nearer.

The Constant Expectancy

One of the interesting things about this parable is that the same virgins that fell asleep are still the same ones who were awakened by the midnight cry. However, we know that the body of Christ has been on the earth for almost two thousand years. What this feature teaches is of great importance. The church, regardless of its point in time over its history, should have constantly expected the return of Christ – in their lifetime, in the coming week, or even in the next passing hour. It is what was meant by the teaching of the Spirit concerning this doctrine. This was to always be a constant expectation of the believer's heart and affections.

Hebrews 9:28

"...so Christ was offered once to bear the sins of many. To those who eagerly wait for Him He will appear a second time, apart from sin, for salvation."

Philippians 3:20-21

"For our citizenship is in heaven, from which we also eagerly wait for the Savior, the Lord Jesus Christ, (21) who will transform our lowly body that it may be conformed to His glorious body, according to the working by which He is able even to subdue all things to Himself."

Romans 8:23-25

"Not only that, but we also who have the firstfruits of the Spirit, even we ourselves groan within ourselves, eagerly waiting for the adoption, the redemption of our body. (24) For we were saved in this hope, but hope that is seen is not hope; for why does one still hope for what he sees? (25) But if we hope for what we do not see, we eagerly wait for it with perseverance."

In all three of these passages the believer/church is taught to eagerly wait for Him to appear. In both Romans and Philippians we are taught to eagerly wait for it with perseverance. The 'for it' refers to the redemption of our body – when we are conformed into the image of His Son (Rom. 8:29). To the Thessalonians when Paul discussed the doctrine of the rapture, he included himself among those who would be alive and remaining (I Thess. 4:17). The first century church was taught to expect His return. This truth is always to be before our minds and ever forming the affections of our heart towards Him.

Even so, come Lord Jesus!

The Spirit and the bride say, "Come!" This should have been the testimony of the church in agreement with the Spirit from the time these words were penned by John. Some of the very last words of Scripture are, *"Surely I am coming quickly." Amen. Even so, come, Lord Jesus!*" (Rev. 22:17, 20) Do we have this eager anticipation for His return? Are we constantly expecting it as the early church was? I know the doctrine was lost in the church world for centuries. The wise and foolish together were asleep, man failing in responsibility. However, the midnight cry has been sounded.

Are we able to say from the depths of our hearts the words, 'even so, come, Lord Jesus?' Or do we have much hesitation in our thoughts? In thinking about our precious Lord's return is it rather, no, not now, do not come yet? I am not ready. My children are not ready. I want grandchildren; I want to see them grow up before me. I have weddings to plan, other things to do, and places to see. Lord, please do not come now! How can this be the proper affections of the heart of the believer? How does this attitude fall in line with the teaching of Scripture? How are these thoughts pleasing to the Lord at all?

The Believer is called according to God's Purpose

The above passage from Romans tells us that 'we were saved in this hope.' God gives us the specific hope of the glorified body conformed to the image of His Son as a definitive purpose and reason for our salvation.

1 Thessalonians 1:9-10

"For they themselves declare concerning us what manner of entry we had to you, and how you turned to God from idols to serve the living and true God, and to wait for His Son from heaven, whom He raised from the dead, even Jesus who delivers us from the wrath to come."

The Thessalonians had turned from idols to God. They were saved for the purpose of serving the living God, and to wait for His Son from heaven. This was their expectation. It was the same in all the early church. They were all taught to wait, expecting the Lord's coming for the church in their lifetime.

The Father would have many sons (Rom. 8:15-16) and He sent the Holy Spirit down to gather them into one body, the body of Christ. In His counsels we are 'the called according to His purpose.' (Rom. 8:28) And this purpose is spelled out for us in no uncertain terms and detail:

Romans 8:29-30

"For whom He foreknew, He also predestined to be conformed to the image of His Son, that He might be the firstborn among many brethren. (30) Moreover whom He predestined, these He also called; whom He called, these He also justified; and whom He justified, these He also glorified."

All is already accomplished in His counsels, and these before time began. It is before the foundations of the world; and it ends with, 'these He also glorified.' We were saved and given life in Christ for this purpose and in this hope. The Father will have His sons. And this should be of the greatest comfort and security for the believer.

The Guarantee of the Indwelling Spirit

If you are saved and possess eternal life, then you have been sealed with the Spirit. He is God's guarantee of these very things (Rom 8:23). God has set in stone a certain determined purpose in His counsels, and He is faithful to do all He wills in accomplishing that exact purpose. He has promised and given us sure and steadfast hopes. He has guaranteed it all by the presence of His Spirit.

2 Corinthians 5:1-5

"For we know that if our earthly house, this tent, is destroyed, we have a building from God, a house not made with hands, eternal in the heavens. (2) For in this we groan, earnestly desiring to be clothed with our habitation which is from heaven, (3) if indeed, having been clothed, we shall not be found naked. (4) For we who are in this tent groan, being burdened, not because we want to be unclothed, but further clothed, that mortality may be swallowed up by life. (5) Now He who has prepared us for this very thing is God, who also has given us the Spirit as a guarantee."

It is all the same teaching. The Spirit given to us is His guarantee of future glory and the heavenly habitation. Presently we groan, being in these earthly bodies (v. 2). We suffer now with Christ, as He suffered in His walk on this earth (Rom. 8:17-18). In this world we have tribulation (John 16:33) and hatred (John 17:14), because we are not of the world and are only strangers here. But the above passage tells us again, that presently as believers, we are to earnestly desire the glorified body. And God has prepared us for this very thing – mortality being swallowed up by life.

The Biblical Truths of the Parable of the Ten Virgins (Matt. 25:1-12)

- The return of the bridegroom is Christ returning for His body, the true church. Even though there are five foolish and five wise virgins looking and acting the same, the parable proves the Lord knows those that are His. The foolish say, "Lord, Lord, open to us!" He replies, "Assuredly, I say to you, I do not know you."

- The ten virgins were five foolish and five wise. This is professing Christianity consisting of wheat and tares

(Matt. 13:24-26). They all have lamps, but the five foolish ones have no seal of the Spirit, no oil. You cannot see the seal of the Spirit; that is why they all look and act the same in the parable, and they are all found together.

- All the virgins fell asleep. To do so they sought out a more comfortable place – all had to be called back out to their original place by the midnight cry (Matt. 25:6). Because all ten sleep together, it is failure in corporate responsibility in the professing church. Many Christian truths are lost while men sleep, and for centuries the church world has not expected the Lord's return. Also while men sleep many tares are given the opportunity to enter into the crop in the field (Matt. 13:25-26). This also allows the growth and spread of corruption and evil, and the spoiling of the crop. This is what has been playing out for centuries in the kingdom of heaven.

- The return of the Lord for His own should be the constant expectation of the believer. The virgins were to remain awake and alert to the coming of the bridegroom. This expectation was to be true for the church in the first century as well as the twenty-first century. It is to be a daily looking for the Lord, and an eager waiting for our glorification. But if any servant says, 'My Master delays his coming...' it is for his own ruin. It also reveals the moral state of his heart as evil.

- The moral state of the kingdom is that all have gone asleep and the coming of the Lord is forgotten by all. The entire reason for the ten virgins going out had been forgotten – this is a commentary on the moral condition of the external professing body. They were no longer waiting for the Lord; although some had oil, none of their lamps were trimmed. It is he who awaits the Lord who watches to be ready to receive Him. All that was manifested was negligence and sleeping. Where was the love for the Lord when no one is occupied with His return? Where is the loyalty to Him? The true character of the believer is formed by the object that governs his heart – waiting for the Lord detaches your heart from this world. Are all the things in our life agreeable to His presence? There is nothing like having the expectation of His coming for us that will search our hearts and govern our conduct.

- The five unwise had to go away to buy oil. This simply shows that it was too late for them to have anything to do with the bridegroom. Also it was too late for the wise to give the unwise any oil. You have to have the oil in order to trim your lamp – this is the rendering of service. Only the wise could do so for the Lord.

- The midnight cry awakens all ten virgins. This doctrine of the rapture has been rediscovered by the church world, the Spirit bringing light to it during the mid-1800s. We are certainly closer today to the return of the bridegroom.

Luke 12:35-37

(35) "Let your waist be girded and your lamps burning; (36) and you yourselves be like men who wait for their master, when he will return from the wedding, that when he comes and knocks they may open to him immediately. (37) Blessed are those servants whom the master, when he comes, will find watching. Assuredly, I say to you that he will gird himself and have them sit down to eat, and will come and serve them."

The Lord is returning and the church will be gathered unto Him. Our waists need to be girded and our lamps burning. We should be constantly waiting and anticipating His return. This is the blessed hope of the church.

Chapter 7: Endnotes

[18] I always contend the Scriptures teach that the only time man's will was truly free was in paradise before the fall. When man was in innocence, he exercised his free will. But when he freely chose to disobey God, sin entered in and became a master over man. Whoever commits sin is a slave of sin (John 8:34), and all men in Adam were doing just that (Rom. 5:12, 19). Man's will was no longer free.

[19] When God gave the law to Israel, He was looking to see if man in Adam could produce righteousness as a fruit before Him. Until this time the question of righteousness in man had not been addressed, not based on the principle of responsibility in man. Abraham was justified by faith – by believing the words and promises God spoke to him (Rom. 4:17-22). God's dealing with Abraham was on the principle of sovereign grace (Rom. 4:13-16). This principle of grace is opposite to that of the principle of responsibility (Rom. 11:6). The doing of the law was based on the principle of responsibility, and man in Adam, or man in the flesh, could not please God. Failure was certain. However, the giving of the law was God specifically looking for the fruit of righteousness. Yet if the law was completed perfectly over one's lifetime, it still only represented human righteousness (Phil. 3:9). The law represented what man in Adam should be before a holy and righteous God, in man's relationships – with God and with his neighbor. This is not the righteousness of God, and never could be, regardless of who was performing the law.

[20] The rejection of the Messiah sent to Israel represents the end of God testing the principle of responsibility in man on his own in the first Adam. Man has not only sinned, but he is a sinner. Man in Adam is condemned. The entire world is condemned (John 12:31). The ending of this last testing can be distinctly seen in two separate scriptures.

Hebrews 9:26 "He then would have had to suffer often since the foundation of the world; but now, once at the end of the ages, He has appeared to put away sin by the sacrifice of Himself."

It was morally the end of the world; sin was complete. All the ages and all the phases of man's probation, after he was chased out of the garden, had been tested. All the privilege and advantage God had given man was found in Israel. Christ appeared at the end when the testing of man in Adam was complete. God had proven by Israel's failure that man in Adam could not produce righteousness as a fruit, and could only be a sinner.

However, at the moral end of the world, God turns to His own working and strength instead of looking at man's work and strength or man's nature and will. The believer's sin has been put away by the sacrifice of Christ. Further, the believer is now the righteousness of God in Christ. This is all based on the principle of sovereign grace. God had to eventually deal with man's sin nature and sins. He could not indefinitely forbear and pass over them (Rom. 3:25). The holy and righteous God would have to be appeased and propitiated, or all mankind would be lost (Rom. 3:19, 23). He deals with man's sin nature and his sins by Christ bearing sins and being made sin; this dealing is according to His own holy and righteous nature. Christ bears the responsibility of man in the first Adam, and God justly condemns Him on the cross (Rom. 8:3). God is no longer passing over, but has now dealt with the problem by an eternally accepted sacrifice, and through the principle of grace. The times of God testing man in the principle of responsibility had come to an end – it was the end of the ages (also see Gal. 4:4 – 'when the fullness of the time had come').

[21] Jesus came to the fig tree and only found leaves. This symbolically represents the law adorning the Jews in the flesh and by outward appearance. The law could not result in life, and therefore no fruit was found in Israel as representing mankind. They were a very privileged people by God, but still could not produce any fruit. Now, the Arminian thought and leaven would say this, "Surely Israel had to produce some fruit. It cannot be this bad. There had to be some fruit on the tree. Surely not all is lost. This has to be a mistake." However, Jesus came to the fig tree and found no fruit – then the tree was judged.

[22] Our individual responsibility as believers stems from our new position as sons of our Father God. Christ is our brother and we are His brethren in the house of God (Gal. 3:26, Heb. 2:10-11, John 8:35-36). We have been placed in the same relationship as Christ – He saying, "...My Father and your Father, and to My God and your God." (John 20:17) We act and speak as sons in the house of our Father. So now we are to emulate how Christ walked on the earth. We are to love the brethren as Christ loved us, giving Himself for us (John 15:12-13, Eph. 5:2, 5:25). We are to be a light to this world as we see that Christ was the light of the world when He was here in it (John 9:5, Eph. 5:8, Phil. 2:15). We are the epistle of Christ before this world (II Cor. 3:3). This is the believer's responsibility as a son with Him.

The principle of responsibility for all who profess Christ (the spoiled crop of wheat and tares) can be seen individually in John 15:1-6. Judaism is the vine of the earth (Rev. 14:18-19). However, Christ is the true vine of God. All the branches that do not bear fruit are the tares in professing Christianity. These cannot light their lamps for they have no oil. They cannot bear fruit for they have no life. They do not abide in the vine at all and therefore do not have the life of the vine flowing to them. The Father takes these away from the vine (v. 2) and they are eventually cast out and wither (v. 6). They will be gathered and burned (judgment).

The branches that bear fruit are the wheat in the crop of professing Christianity. These have eternal life and so have the life of the vine flowing to them. Therefore they are said to abide in the vine and produce fruit (v. 4). The Father prunes these so they bear more fruit (v. 2).

As believers we abide in the vine. As believers we are the wheat. As believers we are the sons of God and we produce 30, 60, 100 fold (Matt. 13:8, 23). As believers we are the branches that produce fruit. We are the branches that are pruned by the Father because the Father loves the sons (Heb. 12:7-11), and they will bear more fruit. We do not abide in the vine by our own strength. We do not abide in Him by stressing and straining and trying hard. These are all foolish Arminian thoughts and teachings, and serve to rob the true believer of security and peace. When was the last time you looked at the branches of a tree and thought these branches are doing a great job in their efforts to just stay attached to the trunk?

Having been justified by faith, we have peace with God (Rom. 5:1) – how is this? It is through our Lord Jesus Christ, not through stressing and straining and good performance. We have this treasure in earthen vessels (II Cor. 4:7) – why? It is so that the excellence of the power may be of God and not of us! When Paul could not be with the Philippians he says, "...work out your own salvation with fear and trembling..." How is this done? It is God who works in you both to will and to do His good pleasure (Phil. 2:12-13). We are believers by the choice and power of God and we are kept by the choice and power of God (John 10:26-29). We are branches that produce fruit. We are the branches that abide in Him, but it is the life from the vine that does the work of producing fruit. "A branch cannot bear fruit of itself... for without Me you can do nothing." It is Christ in us, and we in Him (John 15:5). This is not Arminian teaching. But it is Biblical teaching and the thoughts of God from His Word.

Notes

Chapter 8:
The Moral Implications
of the Doctrine

In the parable of the ten virgins we saw that the professing church has been asleep for centuries. As noted, this is a failure of corporate responsibility – all ten, both foolish and wise, slept and slumbered together. The task defining this responsibility was clear – remain awake and alert, looking for the return of the bridegroom. They did not do this and the church world suffered the results.

Failure in responsibility always has its consequences, and none of these are ever good. Early in its history the professing church lost sight of the doctrine of His return for the church, and with this, lost the earnest expectation and constant vigilance in it. The sleeping allows corruption and evil to enter in, and this grows and ripens to the end. The principles of this age are different from those of the dispensation to come, so we cannot be looking for God to separate things out. The tares are mixed in with the wheat, and the corruption and evil grows and prospers (Matt. 13:28-29).

The Principle of Evil

Genesis 15:16

"But in the fourth generation they shall return here, for the iniquity of the Amorites is not yet complete."

Evil and corruption love to grow, spread, and ripen. It is certainly what weeds (tares) are designed to do all on their own. This goes on to a certain end, as you can see with the Amorites above in Canaan land – until their iniquity was complete.

Matthew 23:29-32

"Woe to you, scribes and Pharisees, hypocrites! Because you build the tombs of the prophets and adorn the monuments of the righteous, and say, 'If we had lived in the days of our fathers, we would not have been partakers with them in the blood of the prophets."

"Therefore you are witnesses against yourselves that you are sons of those who murdered the prophets. Fill up, then, the measure of your fathers' guilt."

The hypocrisy and corruption in Israel among its religious leaders at the time of Jesus' first appearing was the worst in its history up to that point. The scribes and Pharisees sit in Moses' seat, but Jesus warns His disciples and the people of all their deceptions (Matt. 23:1-3). They were to properly obey what they say regarding the law as the leaders of the nation, but they were not to follow their examples. This is another example of how evil grows and ripens to judgment.

This Present Evil World

The outward world is viewed by God in this way – it is ripening in evil to a certain end. The end will come when the Son of Man returns to this earth in judgment of the world (Rev. 1:7, Matt. 24:30). A few years before Christ's return, Satan is cast out of the heavens down to the earth. What this results in is rejoicing in the heavens, but woe to the inhabitants of the earth and the sea, for the devil has come down to you, having great wrath (Rev. 12:12). The last few years of the world before its judgment will be the full display of evil, as never seen before on the face of the earth (Matt. 24:21). The character of the world at this time is one of apostasy, blasphemy, and outright rebellion against God (the character of the dragon cast down to the earth). Certainly in principle, evil in the world is fully ripening to the end.[23]

The Principle of Evil in Professing Christianity

Through failure in corporate responsibility evil also grows, spreads, and ripens in the professing church. Satan is presently in the heavens (above the earth), and he is there for the corruption of the church world. In the heavens he acts like a serpent. The corruption of professing Christianity is by subtlety, worldliness, and false teaching (lies). God will not allow the full display of corruption in the church world at this time, but restrains its greater expression (II Thess. 2:6-8). But the time is coming when the restraints will be removed. Here is an outline of the progression and history of evil in the church world:

1. The mystery of lawlessness starts in the early church in Paul's time (II Thess. 2:7). With the end of the apostolic church begins the steady decline and decay of the professing church.[24] Ephesus will not repent and return to its first position (Rev. 2:5). Christ threatens the removal of its candlestick.

2. For centuries the church world has failed in responsibility. Early on 'wicked servants' established the false teachings of church authority through succession and by these teachings controlled and abused other servants of the Master. The professing church has long been asleep, especially to the blessed hope of the coming of the Lord for His own. In other areas of responsibility we see the professing church building on the earth with wood, hay, and stubble (I Cor. 3:9-13). Also the leaven of false teaching penetrates and saturates the whole lump to the end (Matt.

13:33). The church world does not endure sound doctrine (II Tim. 4:3-4). It has been this way for a long time. These are all areas of corporate failure in its history.

3. All along God has restricted the full display of evil in the church world. However this will not go on much longer. When Christ comes back to remove His body from this world (I Thess. 4:13-18), the restrictions will have ended (II Thess. 2:7). The tares of professing Christianity, bundled together and left behind, will experience a great apostasy from any pretense of Christian truth (II Thess. 2:3, I Tim. 4:1). Laodicea is spewed out of Christ's mouth (Rev. 3:15-17) and the candlestick is finally removed after much patience shown by the Lord.

4. Jezebel in Thyatira is a special failure of responsibility of the professing church as it progresses through time (Rev. 2:20-23). Mystery, Babylon the Great, is professing Christianity as it rides the hidden Roman beast. Her influence, power, and wealth will be destroyed by ten formerly Christianized kingdoms and increasingly apostate kings (Rev. 17). This effectively ends the history of professing Christianity before the judgment of the world. Judgment begins at the house of God, and in the case here, the destruction of all in professing Christianity that pretends to be the false bride of Christ that is left on the earth (I Pet. 4:17).

5. The Roman beast rises out of the bottomless pit (Rev. 17:8). It now takes on the character and behavior of a beast again – having an independent will from God, apostate, blasphemous, and rebellious. It is no longer under the pseudo-Christian influence of the Babylonian whore (Rev. 17:3-6). The man of sin is revealed, who is the son of perdition (II Thess. 2:3). The ten kings give their power to the last Caesar (Rev. 17:10-13), the head of the revived Roman beast. Much of this last point is written to show how the world becomes anti-Christian

and openly apostate after God's judgment of what is left of the church world (Rev. 17:15-17).

The Wicked Servant says in his heart – 'my master delays his coming'

The ten virgins, all sleeping and slumbering, depict the failure in responsibility related to the doctrine of the rapture of the church – the removal of the body of Christ from this world to go into the presence of the Father. The moral implications of this failure can be seen in the comparison of two portions of Scripture.

Luke 12:35-37

"Let your waist be girded and your lamps burning; and you yourselves be like men who wait for their master, when he will return from the wedding, that when he comes and knocks they may open to him immediately. Blessed are those servants whom the master, when he comes, will find watching. Assuredly, I say to you that he will gird himself and have them sit down to eat, and will come and serve them."

Matthew 24:48-49

"But if that evil servant says in his heart, 'My master is delaying his coming,' and begins to beat his fellow servants, and to eat and drink with the drunkards..."

The good servants are waiting and anticipating the return of the Lord. Their waists are girded and their lamps fully burning. They are always looking and ready. But the evil servant is not waiting and anticipating the Lord's return. He says, "My master delays his coming." As a direct result of this thinking and attitude, he enters into two areas of immorality.

- He begins to abuse his fellow servants. This, I would think, symbolizes types of ecclesiastical abuse within the church world. An example of this might be the tenant of faith in Roman Catholicism by which authority and infallibility is passed down through apostolic succession. This is a belief that is completely unscriptural and is the creation of the human mind, serving as a means of control and abuse, all in the name of Christ. It is part and parcel of man exalting himself by Arminian doctrine and the Judaizing of the Christian faith. There are many other forms of this type of abuse.

- He eats and drinks with the drunkards. This is symbolic of the professing church joining with the world. The body of Christ is not of the world. But the greater corporate body of profession solicits the world and joins in an unholy relationship with it. In the prophetic language this is known as fornication and sexual immorality. The joining of the professing church with the world is easily seen in many passages of Scripture.

  1. With Pergamos, the third church, the professing church was drawing closer to the world. Christ says, "I know...where you dwell, where Satan's throne is." They were allowing the worldly doctrines of Balaam to enter in, producing idolatry and sexual immorality (worldliness – Rev. 2:13-15).

  2. With Thyatira, the fourth church (the remarkable form of Romanism), the professing church welcomes Jezebel, the false prophetess, to dwell in it and birth her own children in her evil abominations. She teaches and beguiles, leading into sexual immorality (worldliness) and idolatry. She knows and teaches the doctrines of the depths of Satan, all in the name of Jesus Christ (Rev. 2:20-24).

  3. Mystery, Babylon the Great, is the professing church world (Rev. 17:6). The vision in this chapter is her history, having Christianized the Roman Empire. During her history this woman's influence has been over the many waters (the Gentile masses well beyond the Roman earth). This influence is by the kings of

the earth committing fornication with her and the inhabitants of the earth being made drunk with the wine of her fornication (Rev. 17:1-2). The inhabitants are intoxicated, losing all individual spiritual insight and enlightenment. In John's vision, when she is seen sitting on the beast, she is adorned with earthly glory and wealth as the false bride of Christ. The cup she holds is full of abominations (idolatries) and the filthiness of her fornication (Rev. 17:3-4). Her unholy relationship with the world is obvious.

1 John 2:15-16

"Do not love the world or the things in the world. If anyone loves the world, the love of the Father is not in him. For all that is in the world—the lust of the flesh, the lust of the eyes, and the pride of life – is not of the Father but is of the world."

The testimony of the history of the professing church world is that it falls in love with the world and the things in the world. And it is saying to itself, "My master delays His return." So then there was allowance for all kinds of corruption and worldliness. There is no perceived need for readiness, no need to be alert. There is time to sleep, and time to party. The pressure is off, we can do as we please, and there is no danger. It is pretension, it is worldliness, and it is human arrogance. It is Laodicea saying, "I am rich, have become wealthy, and have need of nothing." Yet it is wretched, miserable, poor, blind, and naked (Rev. 3:17). These are five descriptive words indicative of the abject spiritual state of the church world in its end.

The Moral Consequences of the True Church's Proper Hope

1 John 3:1-3

"Behold what manner of love the Father has bestowed on us, that we should be called children of God! Therefore the world does not know us, because it did not know Him. (2) Beloved, now we are children of God; and it has not yet been revealed

what we shall be, but we know that when He is revealed, we shall be like Him, for we shall see Him as He is. (3) And everyone who has this hope in Him purifies himself, just as He is pure."

Those who have and possess true Christian hopes will purify themselves by these hopes. They are all unseen and in glory, and not of this world or life on earth. Our true hopes serve to set our affections and desires apart from this world, and apart from worldly cares. The character of this doctrine is not of the world, and serves to disentangle and detach us from the things of the world, and in truth, the things of the earth (Phil. 3:18-21). The holding of this doctrine in constant expectation is at once both practical and powerful in accomplishing this task.

Having the lamps trimmed and burning, waiting for the bridegroom, was the responsibility of professing Christianity the entire time of its existence. It is true the Lord tarried and all the virgins in the parable slept (Matt. 25:5). This is indicative of the moral state of the kingdom of heaven – all had forgotten the bridegroom's coming. In the history of the church world even good men failed to teach this truth and to be enlivened by this expectation. What does the slumbering and sleeping say about the professing church's love for the Savior? When all had forgotten Him, was it not that they were getting comfortable in the world? Their lamps weren't trimmed. They weren't ready to receive Him. There was little light at all. Their love and affection for Christ had grown cold.

The Affections of the Believer's Heart

The proper moral state of the believer depends on our constant expectation of this hope: waist girded, lamps burning, and you yourselves be like men who wait for their master to return. *"For where your treasure is, there your heart will be also."* (Luke 12:34) The true character of the professing Christian is established by the object that holds his heart's affections and attention. This object must be the Lord Jesus Christ. The believer's motive for all his conduct must have its basis in his affections for Him and an expectation of Him. There is nothing that truly separates the Christian from this world than waiting for Him. This expectation will search the heart so that nothing will be hidden there that is inappropriate to our being in the Lord's physical presence. What are the many things we cling to down here in this world? Is there anything in your life, in your affections, which would make you wish the Lord's coming be delayed?

Luke 12:37-38

"Blessed are those servants whom the master, when he comes, will find watching. Assuredly, I say to you that he will gird himself and have them sit down to eat, and will come and serve them. And if he should come in the second watch, or come in the third watch, and find them so, blessed are those servants."

This will not be true on the earth, but only in the heavens and with Him in the Father's house. As His faithful brethren – watching and expecting His return – out of His love and affection for them He will serve them in glory. This speaks of the believer's intimate relationship, fellowship, and communion with Him then, unhindered by sin. The watching and waiting for Him develops and intensifies the Christian's fellowship and communion with Him now, where it is always hindered by sin.

The Believer's Responsibility in Service

The question may be lingering, "what about our service for Him now?" Service always speaks to different things such as recompense and reward. It is not the development of fellowship and communion with Him. It is not that we do not have responsibility in this area.

Luke 12:42-44

"And the Lord said, "Who then is that faithful and wise steward, whom his master will make ruler over his household, to give them their portion of food in due season? Blessed is that servant whom his master will find so doing when he comes. Truly, I say to you that he will make him ruler over all that he has."

After the above verses emphasizing the need for watching and waiting by His servants (Luke 12:32-38), Jesus addresses the service. He says, "Blessed is that servant whom his master will find *so doing* when he comes." The servant who is faithful in his doing will be blessed of the Lord. But we can see that this involves the Lord's inheritance we all share with Him, as well as our portion and place in His future government over it.

The idea of recompense and reward is often the opportunity for human thought, pride, and exaltation – a looking at what I can do, or I have done. It is a slippery slope if we do not exercise caution and Scriptural thoughts. *The excellence of the power is of God, and not of us.* This is only applicable when you are actually doing the will of God in the plan and counsels of God. That is why we are only earthen vessels (II Cor. 4:7). *It is God in us, both to will and to do His good pleasure* (Phil. 2:13). But the only things that count are those things which are His good pleasure. And when it comes to labors and payment we cannot be forcing the sovereign God away from the management of the kingdom of heaven (Matt. 20:1-15). God's principle of grace is that the last will be first, and the first last and that many are called, but few are chosen (Matt. 20:16). God blesses according to Himself. It is not a certain amount of labor for a certain amount of reward, as if we are bargaining with God on a price (Matt. 20:10-12). Is it not right for God to do what He wishes with His own things? (Matt. 20:15). So often we forget these things and are not thankful to God for the position we are in.

Proper Christian Hopes govern the Believer's behavior and service

The rapture is the beginning and entrance of the church into the glory. The Lord promised to come for us, so that we might be where He is – with the Father. It is the Father who has given us these hopes and bestowed upon us His love. We are called His children, His sons. Our hope is not realized yet, but we know that it is the Father's desire that we be like Christ, conformed to the image of His Son (Rom. 8:29-30). Such glorious hope will change us even now. While we wait, day by day we behold the glory of God in the face of Jesus Christ, and are changed and transformed into this same image – from glory to glory (II Cor. 3:18).

The doctrine of the rapture of the church was to be a substantive part of the believer's thinking. The moral state of the saints depends on keeping His coming in the affections of their hearts and constantly before their eyes. In its history, the church has declined in spirituality exactly in proportion to the loss of this doctrine, and to the loss of its constant expectancy. As a result, the church has become weak and worldly, with false hopes and unsound teaching.

The Constant Expectancy is the Wisdom of God

Believers who expect the imminent return of the Lord for them simply will live different lives. If you truly expect the Lord to return tomorrow, how will you live this day? If His return for us were a present thought on our hearts and minds, how many things would disappear from around us? How many cares and desires that burden us and distract us from Him would we cast off? With this thought our loins would be girded and our lamps would be burning. And it is the wisdom of God that He intended this truth to be held by all His children, regardless of where on the timeline of the history of the church they fell.[25] The Spirit taught the early church to expect the Lord's return. Paul taught that when the Lord does return, that God will bring with Him those who sleep in Jesus (I Thess. 4:13-14). And again, the Thessalonians were saved in this very hope:

1 Thessalonians 1:9-10

"For they themselves declare concerning us what manner of entry we had to you, and how you turned to God from idols to serve the living and true God, (10) and to wait for His Son from heaven, whom He raised from the dead, even Jesus who delivers us from the wrath to come."

They were saved for what purpose? Surely to serve the living and true God, but also to wait for His Son from heaven. It was part of what the Thessalonians were converted to – the waiting. "...but we also who have the firstfruits of the Spirit, even we ourselves groan within ourselves, eagerly waiting for the adoption, the redemption of our body. For we were saved in this hope..." (Rom. 8:23-24)

The Believer before the Judgment Seat of Christ

2 Corinthians 4:14

"...knowing that He who raised up the Lord Jesus will also raise us up with Jesus, and will present us with you."

1 John 4:17-18

"Love has been perfected among us in this: that we may have boldness in the day of judgment; because as He is, so are we in this world. There is no fear in love; but perfect love casts out fear, because fear involves torment. But he who fears has not been made perfect in love."

We go to the judgment seat of Christ after we are raised up and glorified. It is after the rapture of the church. It will be after the believer is conformed into the image of His Son. We go to the judgment seat of Christ after having been conformed into the image of the Judge we stand before. In this the believer is to have confidence and boldness without tormenting fear – in Christ, as He is, so are we. This is a blessed thought for the believer. It is one without fear or condemnation. This is the blessed hope of the church.

Chapter 8: Endnotes

[23] In principle, evil is always consistent in this way – it grows, spreads, and ripens. We easily see this in the description of the four Gentile world monarchies as beasts (Dan. 7). The fourth beast (the Roman Empire) is described as different from the three preceding it. It is one that is dreadful and terrible, exceedingly strong. It goes forth devouring, breaking in pieces, and trampling the residue. The final form of this fourth beast is worse than its original, as seen as ascending out of the bottomless pit (Rev. 17:8). Its last form is given the dragon's power and his throne (Rev. 13:2). It is an amalgamation of the evil character of the three beasts that preceded it (Rev. 13:2).

[24] Allow me to share an example that may bring some clarity to this principle of evil and the statement by Paul that the mystery of lawlessness was already at work in his day. I am a licensed private pilot with an instrument rating. All pilots know that when traveling to a given destination the attempt is made to fly at a set altitude and on a course that is a relatively straight line. Modern instrumentation, GPS satellite navigation, and integrated autopilots make this task quite different today than what flying was in the past. In the past you had to hand fly the plane, constantly monitoring instruments that were inherently less dependable and accurate, while checking your own skills in maintaining proper altitude and course.

All pilots know that an error at the beginning or an instrument malfunction, even a small less significant one, will only be compounded through the course of the flight, ending in a far greater inaccuracy and problem at the end. They know that this may be devastatingly true with errors in either altitude or direction. In the professing church the mystery (hidden and subtle) of lawlessness was taking root at the beginning. Evil has been growing, spreading, and increasing over the course of time in the corporate body. The evil that had its small beginnings will only be compounded many times by the end.

[25] It is the divine wisdom of God that this doctrine of the rapture of the church be held by all believers. It leads them to having a constant expectation of the event itself. This anticipation then leads the believer to greater purity and holiness (I John 3:1-3). The wisdom of God is that this is true for all believers, regardless of being in the first century or the twenty-first century. It is the same teaching held, and the same earnest expectation properly generated by it. The same virgins that fell asleep

are the same ones aroused at the end. They are the same servants given talents when the master originally departs who have to answer when He returns. The seven churches addressed in Rev. 2-3 were contemporary existing churches in the time of John. I can see along with many other believers that these seven are symbolic of the progressive history of the professing church on the earth. We may get this partially from hindsight. But it still remains that all seven were contemporary churches at the time, and could be viewed in that light by the first century church.

The Lord has delayed His coming, this is a reality. The parable of the virgins tells us directly that when the bridegroom delayed, they all slept. The question is, did the Lord want the early church to constantly expect His coming for them, or did He want them to say, "My master delays His coming."? The evil servant does not deny that his master will eventually return, but he has lost the sense and present expectation of it. Not to be watching was the failure of the church world. The professing church was taught to watch, not to expect a delay. When the Lord says to the seven churches, "Behold, I come quickly," why would it not be the Lord's wisdom to have them believe such? It is always the present hope of the saints. It is wrapped in symbolism, but it is the divine wisdom of God. Naysayers accuse the first century church of making a big mistake. Rather it is the simple understanding of the counsel and wisdom of God taught by His Spirit to the spiritually minded believer. All believers are to constantly expect His coming for the church, regardless of what century they lived in. This is the mind of Christ.

Notes

Chapter 9:

Our Privileged Position

verybody in Christianity knows that the history of the Old Testament scriptures is dominated by God's dealings with the nation of Israel. This starts in Exodus, the second book of Scripture, although the story of the lives of the patriarchs is told in Genesis. The great body of prophetic scripture is found in the Old Testament written by Jewish prophets. They were given a measure of the Spirit from time to time in order to speak the words of God (John 3:34). We do well to note the character and nature of these types of passages.

The Nature and Character of Prophetic Scriptures

- All prophetic scripture is related to Israel. Jehovah mainly deals directly with Israel, but other times indirectly by using the Gentiles as a means of correction or judgment against them. Prophecy revolves around Israel because, in the end, as a people they become the centerpiece of the earthly glory of Jesus Christ.

- Prophecy is about the earth and God's dealings and government of the earth (Dan 4:25, 34-37). Israel is the earthly calling of God and everything in their history and religion connects them to the world. All the promises given to them connect them to the earth and the land, and are certainly earthy in nature. Israel and Jerusalem are the central locations for the future government of God on this earth according to prophecy.

- Prophecy is about the counting of time concerning Israel (Dan. 9:24). And time being counted is only on the earth and about earthly things. Time is not counted in the heavens or with heavenly things.

The Nature and Character of the Gospels and the Book of Acts

A lot of the material in the gospels is related to Israel and God's dealings with them as a people and nation. We see there the story of God sending the Messiah of prophecy to Israel (Matt. 1:21-23), and their rejection of Him (Matt. 27:35-37). They would not have Him as their King, but instead wanted Caesar (John 19:15). In the gospels we see God set Israel aside, their house would remain desolate. This desolation would be for a long time, until this same Jesus, their Messiah, comes to them again and they say, "Blessed is He who comes in the name of the Lord." (Matt. 23:37-39) This setting aside of Israel as a people is told in the gospels and in the book of Acts, if we would have spiritual eyes to see.

Acts 28:23-29

(23) "So when they had appointed him a day, many came to him at his lodging, to whom he explained and solemnly testified of the kingdom of God, persuading them concerning Jesus from both the Law of Moses and the Prophets, from morning till evening. (24) And some were persuaded by the things which were spoken, and some disbelieved. (25) So when they did not agree among themselves, they departed after Paul had said one word: "The Holy Spirit spoke rightly through Isaiah the prophet to our fathers, (26) saying,

'Go to this people and say:

"Hearing you will hear, and shall not understand;
And seeing you will see, and not perceive;
(27) For the hearts of this people have grown dull.
Their ears are hard of hearing,
And their eyes they have closed,
Lest they should see with their eyes and hear with their ears,
Lest they should understand with their hearts and turn,
So that I should heal them."'

(28) "Therefore let it be known to you that the salvation of God has been sent to the Gentiles, and they will hear it!" (29) And when he had said these words, the Jews departed and had a great dispute among themselves."

This is the end of the book of Acts and it is about the blindness of the nation of Israel. It is a definite turning away from Israel by God, and a turning to the Gentiles. My point is that there is a great part of Scripture that involves God's dealings with the nation of Israel. More than we would probably want to admit as Christians. If Israel is involved in so much of this book we hold dear, we would do well then to understand Israel and God's ways in dealing with them. I cannot fathom ever having a thorough comprehension of Scripture without an understanding of God's thoughts and ways toward this people.

The Mind of God towards Israel revealed in Scripture

First we should ask this question – What makes Israel so special to God? Israel has always been a privileged nation; we can all say they are God's chosen people. But what does this mean? Do we have a Biblical understanding of this question and related statements, and do we know God's thoughts and mind concerning Israel?

Deuteronomy 7:6-7

"For you are a holy people to the Lord your God; the Lord your God has chosen you to be a people for Himself, a special treasure above all the peoples on the face of the earth. (7) The Lord did not set His love on you nor choose you because you

were more in number than any other people, for you were the least of all peoples;"

Israel is special to God. This has to be in reference to something that isn't as special to Jehovah. The passage reads, "…above all the peoples on the face of the earth." There it is! Israel is special to God in comparison to all other peoples, all other nations. This is one Biblical understanding, one truth, concerning the mind of God towards Israel. But there are other truths to realize here.

- *The Lord your God has chosen you to be a people for Himself.* They are a chosen people, and chosen by God[26]

- *The Lord did not choose them because they were more in number.* They actually were the least of all peoples. The reason for God choosing Israel was not found in Israel – anything they were, anything they would do, or anything they had done. They were not a great people, but the least of all peoples. God's choice of Israel had nothing to do with Israel, in and of themselves.

- *The reason God chose them is not given.* He set His love on them, but His reasons for doing so are hidden within Himself. One revealed spiritual truth in Scripture concerning the choices God makes is that they all serve to glorify Him, always (Rom. 9:17). But even here we must have a certain understanding. God will be glorified in Israel, not by anything they will do, but by what God does for them in sovereign power and grace (Ez. 36:16-38, 37:21-28).

The Separation of Israel by God

Israel has been a privileged nation. They were a chosen people.[27] They were separated from the Gentiles, God built a wall around them in their religion. But this is what it means, nothing more than this. They were a holy people unto the Lord because they were separated from the Gentiles. But it is important to note scripturally what it was they were not separated from:

1. Israel was not separated from the world. They remained very much a part of this world.

2. Israel was not separated from the flesh. They were never in the Spirit, but rather remained a people in the flesh (John 4:21-23, Rom. 8:8-9). Their unity as a nation was in the flesh – as physical descendants of Abraham with the sign of circumcision in the flesh. Israel never had a walk of faith, but one by sight and senses. Their religion was given to them by God, but it was geared to the flesh. It separated them from the other Gentile gods and false worship, enabling Israel to worship the One true God in a measure of truth, but did not separate them from the flesh.

3. Israel was not separated in position from the first Adam. Israel always remained in Adam and eventually refused a new position in the second Adam. They refused the second Adam altogether. By rejecting Jesus Christ they are rejecting the Father (John 15:21-25) and actually rejecting the God they say they worship (John 8:54-55).

I said all this to show that Israel was a very privileged people. They had the oracles of God (Rom. 3:1-2). They had the promises, the covenants, the law, the tabernacle service, the patriarchs, and Christ coming to them in the flesh (Rom. 9:4-5). The Gentiles had none of this. When we say these things we must maintain the proper scriptural understanding concerning them. This separation is obviously all God, in what He thinks, what He decides, and what He does. It is nothing in Israel and it is everything in God. We must think as God thinks concerning them.

Israel's Future according to the Faithfulness of God

There is coming a future time when God will recognize Israel as His people again. When He does, it will be according to His own faithfulness (Rom. 3:1-4). God will choose a remnant that He will seal and preserve.[28] He will save and form a nation this way, all by His own work. At that time He will fulfill every promise He has ever made to this people, by sovereign power and grace. It will no longer be a testing of the principle of responsibility in Israel. They will produce fruit unto God, but it will be by the principle of divine sovereign power and grace.

The Believer/Church is privileged of God

The believer/church is also in a privileged position, except a much higher one than that of Israel. We have been brought to this by God through faith in the shed blood of Jesus Christ (Rom. 3:25). It is similar to Israel in that it is all by the sovereign choice and grace of God. It was nothing in us, nothing we had done or would do. God will never allow any boasting, not in Israel and not in the church. It is all God's work. We are God's workmanship, created by Him, created in Christ Jesus (Eph. 2:10).

John 1:12-13

"But as many as received Him, to them He gave the right to become children of God, to those who believe in His name: who were born, not of blood, nor of the will of the flesh, nor of the will of man, but of God."

These verses should suffice to show conclusively that the believer is in his new position by the sovereign work of God. We are born of God. Children of God are not born of blood – that would be natural birth and in Adam. Children of God are not born by the will of the flesh or by the will of man – this would be man's decisions and choices. Similar to God's choice of Israel, the believer is chosen by God in sovereign grace.

The Believer's Position in Christ

That seems to be where the similarities between God's choice of Israel and His choice of the believer end. The position we have been given as believers is greater than that of Israel in every way. We have an association with Jesus Christ, the very Son of the living God. We are not of this world. We have no relationship with the world and have been set apart from it. Our relationships are all new. They are with Christ and with the Father God. Our associations, relationships, and position are all different now. These things are present realities of the believer's placement 'in Christ.' And in these truths we have been privileged with brighter and more blessed purposes in Christ. What is this new position for the believer/church?

John 20:17

"Jesus said to her, "Do not cling to Me, for I have not yet ascended to My Father; but go to My brethren and say to them, 'I am ascending to My Father and your Father, and to My God and your God.'"

The Believer's position is the Son of Man's position

There should be no doubt in the believer's mind that this passage describes his new position in Christ Jesus. The association with Him is contained in His language. The new relationships are clearly defined by His words. The new position for the believer is the same position that the Son of God has as the Son of Man raised from the dead. His Father, as the Son of God, is our Father, as the sons of God in Him (Gal. 3:26). His God, as the Son of Man, is our God – this is established by our being crucified with Christ (Gal. 2:20, Rom. 6:6), dying with Him (Rom. 6:8, Col. 2:20, 3:3), buried with Him (Rom. 6:4, Col. 2:12), and then being raised from the dead with Him (Col. 2:12, Col. 3:1, Eph. 1:19-20, 2:5). Further, Christ calls us brethren. We are brothers together, and sons with Him. This is our new position. This is the privileged position of the believer.

1.) The believer is born of God (John 1:13), and therefore we are the new creation of God in Christ (II Cor. 5:17, Col. 3:10, Eph. 4:24). It is Christ living in us; the life we have is Christ (Gal. 2:20, Col. 3:3-4). We are partakers of the divine nature – a nature necessary to even have a relationship with God, and to enjoy that relationship in fellowship and communion with Him.

2 Peter 1:2-4

"Grace and peace be multiplied to you in the knowledge of God and of Jesus our Lord, (3) as His divine power has given to us all things that pertain to life and godliness, through the knowledge of Him who called us by glory and virtue, (4) by which have been given to us exceedingly great and precious promises, that through these you may be partakers of the divine nature, having escaped the corruption that is in the world through lust."

Is this not a privileged position? We partake of the nature of God. The life in us is Jesus Christ, and that life is the resurrected life of the Son of Man raised from the dead. God has given to us all things concerning this divine life and nature (godliness). Our calling is to glory. The privilege and promises are exceedingly great and precious!

> 2.) As the Son of Man raised up and exalted on high, Christ re-enters the glory of God. All the glory He receives as the Son of Man He shares with the believer (John 17:22). Then He says this:

John 17:24

"Father, I desire that they also whom You gave Me may be with Me where I am, that they may behold My glory which You have given Me; for You loved Me before the foundation of the world."

The Believer's Association with Christ – wonderful privilege

His fervent desire is not to be alone. Do we remember what He said earlier in this gospel? *"The hour has come that the Son of Man should be glorified. Most assuredly, I say to you, unless a grain of wheat falls into the ground and dies, it remains alone; but if it dies, it produces much grain."* (John 12:23-24) The Son of Man will not be alone. Christ's desire is for the believer/church to be with Him where He is, to behold His glory and to share in it with Him. We know this will be by the rapture of the church. Our bodies will be glorified and we will be caught up into the clouds to meet the Lord in the air, and thus, we will always be with the Lord.

Beyond this, when the Scriptures speak of Christ being manifested (appearing) to the world, we know it is for the judgment of the world. But His appearing is with glory, and the church will appear (manifested) to the world with Him, in this glory (Col. 3:4). This is the earthly glory of Jesus Christ, the Son of Man. We easily see then, from the Scriptures, that we share in the heavenly glory of Christ having been physically taken to the Father's house, and also rule and reign in the earthly glory of Christ, being manifested with Him to the world.

Our associations with Christ have brought us into wonderful privilege. We are blessed by the Father with every spiritual blessing in the heavens (Eph. 1:3). The Father Himself chose us (Eph. 1:4). The Father Himself predestined us in His love (Eph. 1:5), and enabled us as acceptable to Him in His beloved Son (Eph. 1:6). Being placed in Christ, we have obtained an inheritance. It is the same inheritance the Father gives to His Son (Heb. 1:2), for we are brethren together with Him, all the sons of the Father (Eph. 1:11, Gal. 4:6-7, Rom. 8:14-17, Col. 1:12).

The Rapture – the Believer's Privilege in Christ

These Biblical truths show us the reality of our associations, relationships, and new position. There is profound spiritual privilege connected to these things. It is in accordance with our spiritual privilege that the Lord will come for us. We will be gathered together to Him, and the church will physically depart this world (I Thess. 4:13-18, II Thess. 2:1). To deny the doctrine of the rapture of the church is to deny the existence of all this spiritual privilege. It is also to deny our proper relationship and association with Him.

John 17:14

"I have given them Your word; and the world has hated them because they are not of the world, just as I am not of the world."

THE BLESSED HOPE OF THE CHURCH

We are privileged to depart this world under the same principles and in the same manner in which Christ departed this world. The believer is not of it, just as He is not of it. Our place is not in this world, but we are already seated in heavenly places in Him (Eph. 2:6). By principle and privilege we will be brought there in physical presence. Before He departed He said He was going away to prepare a place for us in the Father's house (John 14:2-3). These are the places He prepares – they are in the heavens. So then the church is not expecting Christ's appearing to this world in judgment, as if we will still be here just like this evil world. No! We are expecting His coming for us, and our gathering together unto Him.

The True Church is not of the Earth

The denial of this doctrine serves to bring the church's hopes and affections from the heavens down to this earth. She (the church, the bride of Christ) will not be seeking those things above, where Christ is, sitting at the right hand of God (Col. 3:1-2). Rather she will set her mind on things on the earth and her affections and life will be found here. She will become part of the world. This is the moral decline and decay of the professing church. To the degree the church world has lost sight of His coming, its earnest expectation, and the teaching of the rapture, is the extent to which she has grown apostate. The true holding of the doctrine in earnest is what keeps the believer/church separated from the world.

Christ is Head, Firstborn, Firstfruits, and Forerunner for the True Church

Our association with Christ is that He is the firstborn among many brethren (Rom. 8:29). He is the forerunner for us, entering in behind the veil in the heavens (Heb. 6:19-20). Jesus Christ is the one who will bring many sons to glory (Heb. 2:10). We are the body of Christ of which He is the Head. We are the bride and He is the Bridegroom. The church is the fullness of the One who fills all things (Eph. 1:22-23, 4:10). The Son of Man risen from the dead is the firstfruits of our brethren who have fallen asleep (I Cor. 15:20). So then:

1 Corinthians 15:23

"But each one in his own order: Christ the firstfruits, afterward those who are Christ's at His coming."

He is coming for the church. It is the privilege of our association and relationship with Him. He is coming for those who are His. This is the rapture of the church. This is the believer's proper hope and constant expectation.

Chapter 9: Endnotes

[26] The sovereign choice of God in Israel, the physical descendants of Abraham, can easily be traced in the Scriptures. *"For they are not all Israel who are of Israel, nor are they all children because they are the seed of Abraham; but, 'In Isaac your seed shall be called.' That is, those who are the children of the flesh, these are not the children of God; but the children of the promise are counted as the seed."* (Rom. 9:6-8) There are actually two types of seed in Abraham being spoken of here, the physical line and the spiritual line. Both center on God's choice of Isaac. The physical line of the true Israel would be called through Isaac instead of Ishmael, the other son. *"For this is the word of promise: 'At this time I will come and Sarah shall have a son."* (Rom. 9:9) For the spiritual line – the children of God – Isaac serves as a type prefiguring Abraham's one true Seed, who is Christ (Gal. 3:16, Heb. 11:17-19). For the spiritual line, this is where the tracing stops – in Christ – and goes no farther. The believer/church is the spiritual seed. The believer/church is 'in Christ.' (Gal. 3:26-29) It was in the one Seed of Abraham that the covenant of promise was confirmed.

God's choice in the physical line is highlighted again by His choice of Jacob over Esau in the third generation. The explanation is stated, *"...that the purpose of God according to election might stand, not of works but of Him (God) who calls..."* (Rom. 9:10-14) This is simply the sovereign will of God shown in His choice of Jacob over Esau, without allowance for any Arminian explanation to the contrary. As God, He has the right to make choices in His will. And when He does make any choice, He remains absolutely righteous in doing so – What shall we say then? Is there unrighteousness with God? (Rom. 9:14) The Biblical answer to this accusation is 'certainly not'; there is no unrighteousness in God. But what is the Biblical explanation?

First, all should realize that unrighteousness in God is an impossibility. God could not be God or remain God if unrighteousness could ever be found in Him. It is foreign to the entire nature and character of God. We're speaking of the one true God here, not some Greek or Roman mythology. If you can conceive of the possibility of some measure of unrighteousness in God, then you simply, like the Jews, do not know the God you say you worship (John 8:54-55). But the explanation must go farther than this.

If you hold the Arminian leaven this passage of Scripture becomes difficult to accept. It goes against the foundational elements of what you believe as realities in Christianity. This entire passage is against the Arminian thought that the 'free will' of man is the all-powerful determining factor of destiny, that the will of the creature trumps the will of God, and that by reasoning, seeking, calculating, and weighing out all options, by the use of his intellect and faculties, man makes his decisions out of his own will that God then is forced to honor. Yet the very next verse in Romans says this, *"For He says to Moses, "I will have mercy on whomever I will have mercy, and I will have compassion on whomever I will have compassion."* (Rom. 9:15) It is the sovereign God's choice. It is His decision. He doesn't abdicate it to man.

Why is there no unrighteousness in God? Because all mankind is utterly depraved and totally lost. And this again is another issue in the Arminian leaven. To believe as they do this cannot be the true state and condition of man. They want to reason, "There is good in man and I have seen it. He cannot be that bad, he is not totally lost. He can seek God, and under the right conditions and circumstances, He does seek after God. He is not a total slave to sin, not totally, just partially. He has a free will and He can decide. He can made good decisions." Yet man in Adam *is* a slave to sin. I do not doubt that he continues to make decisions, and he thinks he does so freely, but if he is a slave, how is he free? If he is a slave to sin, how can he be seeking God? Is sin and God the same thing? If sin is man's master, it will not allow him to seek a new one. There is none that seek after God, no, not one. (Rom. 3)

If man is utterly depraved as the Scriptures conclusively teach, then all men are guilty and under the sentence of death, condemnation, and wrath from God (Rom. 3:19, 5:18). How then is God unrighteous for entering into this situation and acting by His own will and purposes? On top of this, His choice to enter in is motivated by His love (Rom. 5:8). How is this unrighteousness? If God did not act, all is lost! How can there be an accusation against God? Is it because it is not universal salvation? The next verse in Romans reads, *"So then it is not of him who wills, nor of him who runs, but of God who shows mercy."* (Rom. 9:16)

[27] The principle of the calling of God in Israel as a people and a nation, as the chosen people of God, is presently set aside by God. If God said, "You are not my people, and I am not your God," the principle of God's calling of them is set aside (Hosea 1:9). In 70 AD the city and temple were destroyed and the Jews that survived were scattered into the nations, not recognized by God as His people, but to live there as the unbelieving Gentiles. Not to worry – the gifts and callings of God are without repentance (Rom. 11:29). In the end He takes earthly Israel again as His people, pouring His Spirit

out on a remnant, and forming a nation from them. On the earth, in the millennium, they will be God's people again. The principle of the calling of God will return again to Israel at that time. God will again acknowledge Israel as His people.

The principle of calling is presently in the forming of the body of Christ by the Holy Spirit sent down from heaven. It is not another earthly calling of a different nation by earthly promises, but a heavenly calling of individuals out of this world, and seated in heavenly places in Christ. For God to turn back to Israel, the earthly calling, He will have to remove the true church from the earth. God does not deal with two different callings at the same time. That is why Israel was set aside when they rejected their Messiah. God would reveal His mystery, send down the Holy Spirit to gather the body, and by the rapture of the church take her into the heavens. He then can and will turn His attention back to Israel and the judging of this world.

[28] The elect of Jesus' prophecies is the Jewish remnant in the end, not the church (Matt 24:22-24, 31, Luke 18:7, Mark 13:20, 22, 27). I cannot stress this point enough. When teachers make the elect in these prophetic passages to be the church, it violates scriptural principles in a serious way. The difference between the two carries all the weight of the scriptural differences between the earthly calling and the heavenly calling. Jesus is speaking prophetically, standing as a Jewish prophet, an Old Testament prophet if you will. Nothing He says disagrees with Old Testament prophecy, nor does it reveal anything different from Old Testament writings, other than a greater progression of understanding of the prophecies themselves. He cannot be referencing the church at all. This would violate the scriptural principle that surrounds prophecy – it is always about Israel, the earth, and God's government of the earth in view of how the Gentiles nations treat Israel. Prophecy is about Israel and the earth. The body of Christ is Christ, and of the heavens alone. In Christ there are no nations – that is a principle of the earth and of prophecy.

Notes

Chapter 10:

His Father and Our Father

The Son of God took on human flesh and came into this world. It was always a point of faith emphasized by Jesus that we understand and believe that He was sent by His Father. This was the eternal Son, described as always in the bosom of the Father, now sent into the world with a mission to accomplish. He was sent by the Father to reveal and declare the Father.

John 1:18

"No one has seen God at any time. The only begotten Son, who is in the bosom of the Father, He has declared Him."

If the Father was to be shown to the world there was only one who could accomplish this task — the very Son of God. No man could do this. No man has seen God at any time. No man has ever ascended up into the heavens to bring this knowledge back down to men on the earth (John 3:13). The truth on this matter is that man could not possibly have this knowledge, this divine knowledge. It would require divinity to reveal divinity, and to do so properly and perfectly.

Matthew 11:27

"All things have been delivered to Me by My Father, and no one knows the Son except the Father. Nor does anyone know the Father except the Son, and the one to whom the Son wills to reveal Him."

Only the Son truly knows the Father, and only the Father truly knows the Son. We have to see and realize that the source of His words is His intimate relationship with the Father as the Son. This relationship is filled with affections and love, His for the Father and the Father for the Son.

The Revelation of the Father is only a Christian truth

Another point to be made from this passage is the explicit truth that the entire revelation of the Father by the Son is a Christian thing. It is a believer thing. No one could know the Father except the ones to whom Jesus Christ the Son chose and willed to reveal Him. This is not Israel's privilege by any stretch of the imagination. Israel is a people and a nation who do not honor the Son, and therefore do not honor the Father who sent Him (John 5:23). They are the people Jesus was specifically referencing when He said:

John 15:21-25

"But all these things they will do to you for My name's sake, because they do not know Him who sent Me. (22) If I had not come and spoken to them, they would have no sin, but now they have no excuse for their sin. (23) He who hates Me hates My Father also. (24) If I had not done among them the works which no one else did, they would have no sin; but now they have seen and also hated both Me and My Father. (25) But this happened that the word might be fulfilled which is written in their law, 'They hated Me without a cause.'"

Israel was guilty of not knowing the One who sent Jesus (v. 21). They are the ones whom He came and spoke to, and are now without excuse (v. 22). They are the ones who hate the Son, and, in a sense, by the law of transitivity are guilty of hating the Father (v. 23). Jesus performed His Father's works in the midst of this nation (v. 24), and their rejection of Him is the proof of their hatred. Israel is the nation with the law, wherein it is said, "They hated Me without a cause." It is abundantly clear who He is speaking of.

I say all this to bring out a few important Biblical realities and truths. The revelation of the Father is not Israel's. Jesus has proven that they actually hate the Father who sent the Son. He proves that they do not even know Him (John 8:54-55). This is Israel's condition then, and it is their position that continues to this day. The revelation of the Father is to the sons by the Son of God. It is truly a believer thing. It is the believer who is chosen by Jesus out of this world (John 15:19). It is the believer to whom Jesus choses to reveal the Father (Matt. 11:27). For that matter, the giving of the Comforter (the Holy Spirit – John 15:26) is emphatically a Christian thing. These things serve to separate us from Israel, not join us to them, or make us like them.

The Corrupting of the Christian World

Are we grafted in to Israel? The last time I heard this teaching that we, as believers, are in fact grafted in to Israel, the entire audience responded with enthusiastic approval. And the Judaizing of the Christian faith marches on. It is the leaven penetrating throughout to the end in the professing Christian world. It was an evil that took root early on in the church, and it will not go away. It will only worsen in its subtle corruption of the Christian faith. This is a false doctrine and it is the root of the corruption of the church world. Those that teach it display their ignorance of church doctrine and truth. We are not Israel. We are not grafted in to Israel. We are the body of Christ exalted into the heavens to the very right hand of God, far above all principality and power and might and dominion (Eph. 1:19-23). We would have to forfeit our Christian position, our relationship with the Father, and all Christian privilege in order to believe such doctrine. All our proper Christian hopes would be rendered lies and our Christian calling lost. (The olive tree of Romans 11:17 is not the nation of Israel)

The Obedience of the Son of God

Jesus, as the Son of God, perfectly revealed the Father. He did this as sent by the Father and revealed only the Father in a very specific display of obedience. It is unique because it was God choosing to be obedient, the Son of God to the Father. Jesus Christ took on flesh and came into this world and always chose, as the Son, to take the role of a servant to His Father. In this way His own will, as the Son, is moved out of the way, and He only and always did the will of the Father. Therefore He only revealed the Father, and did so perfectly.

John 12:44-45

"Then Jesus cried out and said, "He who believes in Me, believes not in Me but in Him who sent Me. And he who sees Me sees Him who sent Me."

It is a point of faith that we believe He was sent by God, and then as the Son, believe He was sent by the Father to reveal the Father. If we believe in Him, then we believe in the God who sent Him. More than this, if we see the Son, then we see the Father whom the Son reveals.[29]

John 14:7-11

"If you had known Me, you would have known My Father also; and from now on you know Him and have seen Him."

(8) Philip said to Him, "Lord, show us the Father, and it is sufficient for us."

(9) Jesus said to him, "Have I been with you so long, and yet you have not known Me, Philip? He who has seen Me has seen the Father; so how can you say, 'Show us the Father'? (10) Do you not believe that I am in the Father, and the Father in Me? The words that I speak to you I do not speak on My own authority; but the Father who dwells in Me does the works. (11) Believe Me that I am in the Father and the Father in Me, or else believe Me for the sake of the works themselves."

The Believer's need for the Indwelling Spirit

There is no doubt that Jesus is a bit disappointed with His disciples. He was with them for three and a half years, tirelessly revealing the Father to them according to His mission as the Son. Yet they still have not grasped it after all this time. This really shows the vital role and necessity for the Holy Spirit to be sent down from heaven to them. They would not understand until the Spirit of truth was dwelling in them (John 14:17). Then we see and understand why He said it was imperative that He depart from them, for unless He left this world, the Helper could not come (John 16:7, 13-15, 7:39).

We know that, as believers, we have been given the Holy Spirit. We have been sealed with the Spirit of sonship by the Father. He is the Spirit of truth dwelling in us now, and He will abide with us forever (John 14:16-17). I hope you will also realize that we are in a different position than the disciples were in, in reference to the above passage. The revealer of truth lives in us (I Cor. 2:9-16). He was not yet dwelling in the disciples in the above passage when they ask, "Lord, show us the Father." You should be able to see the difference that this makes.

John 16:25

"These things I have spoken to you in figurative language; but the time is coming when I will no longer speak to you in figurative language, but I will tell you plainly about the Father."

The same spiritual understanding is present in this passage. In the disciples' present state it was not possible for them to fully grasp the truth. They simply couldn't. The Lord's physical presence with them could only bring them so far as for spiritual truth and revelation. In their present spiritual state, Jesus was with them and the Spirit was with them, but the Spirit wasn't in them (John 14:17). They were brought to a place far better than unbelieving Israel, but not yet in the position of the Holy Spirit dwelling in the believer.

Israel's Position is 'of the World' and 'in Adam' and 'in the flesh'

- The position of unbelieving Israel, as revealed throughout the entire gospel of John, is described by the Holy Spirit as being 'of the world.' (John 8:23, 17:14) It is equal to all mankind's position in the first Adam. It is the spiritual state of being 'in the flesh.' (Rom. 8:8-9) and not having the Holy Spirit dwelling in them. It is also described in the gospel of John as being 'not of God' and 'not of My sheep.'

John 8:47

"He who is of God hears God's words; therefore you do not hear, because you are not of God."

To clearly see the spiritual position of Israel described in this verse you must pay attention to the sequence of His words. He tells Israel, "...you do not hear, *because* you are not of God." It would be a very different thought, and even an Arminian thought, if it was switched around to say, "...you are not of God, because you do not hear." *Their spiritual position is 'not of God.'* Given this spiritual state in Adam, they simply cannot hear the words of God.

This is an important spiritual understanding concerning all mankind by birth in Adam, including the nation of Israel He is speaking to. He is not talking to them about their human efforts to understand or their willingness to hear. That is the Arminian spin of human achievement that simply would require reversing the placement of the phrases He uses in the above verse. He is not speaking of him who wills, or of him who runs, but instead, the human position by birth in Adam (Rom. 9:16). Their position in Adam is 'not of God.' Therefore it is not possible for them to hear God's words.

John 10:26-27

"But you do not believe, because you are not of My sheep, as I said to you. My sheep hear My voice, and I know them, and they follow Me."

Once again the sequence of His words is paramount for a proper understanding of Israel's condition in the first Adam. He says to Israel, "...you do not believe, because you are not My sheep." It would have an entirely different meaning if He said, "...you are not my sheep, because you do not believe." Again, this latter would be the Arminian leaven that has its own tentacles spreading out through all of Christendom. It penetrates secretly to the end, and will saturate all (Matt 13:33). It will taint all Christian doctrine, because it exalts the power of man and robs the glory of God.

The Disciples Position before the Resurrection

- The position of the disciples while Christ was physically with them and before the resurrection was one of being personally chosen by Him and set apart from the world. They were quickened by Him and had eternal life. They were not in the first Adam anymore and they were not of the world.

John 15:19

"If you were of the world, the world would love its own. Yet because you are not of the world, but I chose you out of the world, therefore the world hates you."

John 5:25-26

"Most assuredly, I say to you, the hour is coming, and now is, when the dead will hear the voice of the Son of God; and those who hear will live. For as the Father has life in Himself, so He has granted the Son to have life in Himself..."

John 17:1-3

"Jesus spoke these words, lifted up His eyes to heaven, and said: "Father, the hour has come. Glorify Your Son, that Your Son also may glorify You, (2) as You have given Him authority over all flesh, that He should give eternal life to as many as You have given Him. (3) And this is eternal life, that they may

know You, the only true God, and Jesus Christ whom You have sent."

They believed in Jesus Christ as the Son of God sent by the Father. They also were convinced that He was the promised Messiah to Israel, and were very much expecting the Messianic kingdom according to prophecy. This was basically the degree of revelation and faith they had at this time. Their understanding did not include His suffering, death, and resurrection, even at this late point in His earthly ministry and after laboriously attempting to forewarn them (Luke 18:31-34). They would have to see with their eyes His suffering, death, and resurrection before they would believe.

The Disciples Position after the Resurrection, yet before Pentecost

- When Jesus was raised up from the dead and showed Himself, the disciples' faith was now in the resurrected Son of Man. He is the Son of God, as the Son of Man raised from the dead. In this He is the one true Seed of Abraham (Gal. 3:16), of which Isaac is a type prefiguring (Heb. 11:17-19). By faith in Jesus Christ, the raised Seed, we are all made sons of God (Gal. 3:26-29). Therefore at His resurrection He calls us brethren for the first time (John 20:17). We are all sons 'in Christ' – the one Begotten Son. This term for Christ as the Begotten Son of God refers to His resurrection (Acts 13:33-34, Heb. 1:5). This is the day all believers became the sons of God (Eph. 2:4-6, Rom. 4:24). We were all baptized into Christ and therefore have put on Christ (Gal. 3:27). We are Christ's, and therefore we are Abraham's seed.

Romans 1:3-4

"...concerning His Son Jesus Christ our Lord, who was born of the seed of David according to the flesh, and declared to be the Son of God with power according to the Spirit of holiness, by the resurrection from the dead."

There is a great connection and association between Christ being declared the Son of God by resurrection from the dead and believers becoming the sons of God in Him. The emphasis of His words immediately after His resurrection is about His relationship and our relationship with the Father.

John 20:17

"Jesus said to her, "Do not cling to Me, for I have not yet ascended to My Father; but go to My brethren and say to them, 'I am ascending to My Father and your Father, and to My God and your God.'"

The Sons of God with the Father

As I said in a previous chapter, this is the clear establishing of the new position of the believer. It is the same position that Christ has as raised from the dead. The basis of the believer's faith is now in a shed blood and an eternal sacrifice of infinite value. And it all points to the position of this Man as *representing* our new position before God. This is Jesus Christ, the Son of God as the Son of Man. It is the Son of God declared so by the resurrection from the dead. It is God saying, *"You are My Son, Today I have begotten You."* (Heb. 1:2-5, Acts 13:33-34) It is this specific relationship between the Father and the Son. But the Son was raised up for our justification, not His (Rom. 4:25). It is the spiritual reality of the many sons of God found in Him and raised up in Him. It is now the relationship between the Father and the many sons 'in Christ.' These are the many sons of the Father destined for glory, and Jesus Christ, the author of their salvation, bringing them there (Heb. 2:10).

The desire of our Affections

I will not be able to adequately express to you the lengths, the widths, the heights, and depths of our now established relationship as sons of God with the Father. The ways and means of establishing this were the Father's own counsels and execution, displaying His goodness toward the believer in Christ. He becomes the substance of our joy, the rest for our souls, the true object of all our hopes, and the desire of our affections. Such is the Father to the believer.

In one sense all Christians are the same in this relationship as sons, with equal privilege to all. But if we speak of our fellowship and communion through the Spirit He has given us, then we speak of something that is intimate and distinct to each one of the individual sons. I cannot copy and duplicate what you have with the Father and Son, as you cannot copy and duplicate me. We are all sons individually, and this is before our entrance into the body of Christ corporately.

John 8:42

"Jesus said to them, "If God were your Father, you would love Me, for I proceeded forth and came from God; nor have I come of Myself, but He sent Me."

John 8:28-29

"Then Jesus said to them, "When you lift up the Son of Man, then you will know that I am, and that I do nothing of Myself; but as My Father taught Me, I speak these things. And He who sent Me is with Me. The Father has not left Me alone, for I always do those things that please Him."

John 10:15-17

"As the Father knows Me, even so I know the Father; and I lay down My life for the sheep. And other sheep I have which are not of this fold; them also I must bring, and they will hear My voice; and there will be one flock and one shepherd."
"Therefore My Father loves Me, because I lay down My life that I may take it again."

John 10:27-30

"My sheep hear My voice, and I know them, and they follow Me. And I give them eternal life, and they shall never perish; neither shall anyone snatch them out of My hand. My Father,

who has given them to Me, is greater than all; and no one is able to snatch them out of My Father's hand. I and My Father are one."

John 10:36-38

"...do you say of Him whom the Father sanctified and sent into the world, 'You are blaspheming,' because I said, 'I am the Son of God'? If I do not do the works of My Father, do not believe Me; but if I do, though you do not believe Me, believe the works, that you may know and believe that the Father is in Me, and I in Him."

John 12:44-45

"Then Jesus cried out and said, "He who believes in Me, believes not in Me but in Him who sent Me. And he who sees Me sees Him who sent Me."

John 12:49-50

"For I have not spoken on My own authority; but the Father who sent Me gave Me a command, what I should say and what I should speak. And I know that His command is everlasting life. Therefore, whatever I speak, just as the Father has told Me, so I speak."

All the above passages were spoken in front of Israel. It was the Son sent into the world and to Israel to testify concerning His Father. He speaks often about His Father in the gospel of John. This is where the revelation of the Father to the believer is almost exclusively found. When He speaks to Israel about the Father, it is a testimony against them – that they do not know the God that they say they worship (John 7:28-29, 8:19, 42, 54-55). When He speaks to the disciples about Him, it is in view of His intimate relationship with His Father, and their association with Him in this position (John 14:20-23, 17:20-26). This is a clear distinction and beautiful insight laid out for us by the Holy Spirit in this gospel, and it is my prayer that all believers see it and grasp the importance of its meaning (John 16:27).

The Dependence and Obedience of the Son of God

The Son came, not to show or do His own will, but to be obedient as a servant to the Father, and to do only the will of His Father. He speaks the words His Father gave Him to speak (John 7:16-18, 8:26, 12:49, 17:8). He does only the works He sees His Father doing (John 5:19-20, 36, 9:4, 10:37-38). If you've seen Him, you have seen the Father (John 12:45, 14:9). The Father was in Him, and He was in the Father (John 10:38, 14:10). The Father was always with Him and never left Him (John 8:29, 16:32), except for His time on the cross (Matt. 27:46). After His work of redemption was finished, He commits His spirit into His Father's hands (Luke 23:46). It is the revelation of the Father by the Son, and speaks volumes of His relationship with His Father.

John 17:23

"I in them, and You in Me; that they may be made perfect in one, and that the world may know that You have sent Me, and have loved them as You have loved Me."

We are associated with Christ. We are His brethren. We are all sons together with Him and of the Father. His Father is our Father. Our Father loves us as He loves His very own Son. How can we imagine anything better than this? The very same love the Father has for His Son, Jesus Christ, is the same He has for you and me. In light of all these truths and this incredible revelation of the Father's love, what should our proper affections and desires be for Him? Would it not be that we would earnestly look forward to the time when we would depart this world and go to be with the Father?

John 14:27-28

"Peace I leave with you, My peace I give to you; not as the world gives do I give to you. Let not your heart be troubled, neither let it be afraid. You have heard Me say to you, 'I am going away and coming back to you.' If you loved Me, you would

rejoice because I said, 'I am going to the Father,' for My Father is greater than I."

Going to the Father

Jesus knows that His departing from His disciples would be upsetting to them. He gives them His peace. It is related to His previous promise to them: having departed this world from them, He would return for them. His departing this world is all about going to His Father (John 16:10, 16). This very thought is exciting to Him. If they loved Him, they would be excited for Him as well. The Father was always with Him, the Father was always in Him, and He in the Father. But there still was a difference, when He was in this world. The Son was about to depart and return to the Father. And this was exciting.

John 14:1-3

"Let not your heart be troubled; you believe in God, believe also in Me. In My Father's house are many mansions; if it were not so, I would have told you. I go to prepare a place for you. And if I go and prepare a place for you, I will come again and receive you to Myself; that where I am, there you may be also."

The sons are going to the Father – this is what this passage is about. Jesus Christ, the one Son, will be sent back to physically gather all His brethren and bring them into His Father's presence. He will be sent by the Father because of how the Father loves us as He does His Son. It is the many sons going to the Father's house. The one Son has gone ahead there and prepared it all. This is about our relationship with the Father. It is about the privilege we have as sons. It is for the reason that now we are Christ's brethren, sons with Him, and we go to His Father and our Father, to His God and ours. This is the blessed and sure hope of all the sons of God. This is the blessed hope of the church.

The Position of all Disciples after Pentecost

- There is a final position of the believer on the earth which became a reality after the day of Pentecost when the Comforter was sent. The Holy Spirit would now be living in them (John 14:17). They would all be sealed by the Holy Spirit (Eph. 1:13). This is what Jesus referred to by the phrase, 'in that day.' They now possessed the Spirit of truth dwelling in them, who would lead them into all truth. And one final spiritual reality concerning Pentecost and their corporate standing; they were all by one Spirit baptized into one body – the body of Christ (I Cor. 12:13). I will add by saying 'on the earth' because we presently are on a walk in the wilderness.

The Believer's Glorified Position after the Rapture

- Our position in the heavens after the rapture of the church is different – it is a glorified state, the end of our salvation, and truly a final and eternal position in Christ. Individually, it is every believer conformed into the image of the Father's Son (Rom. 8:29). Corporately, it is a glorious church without spot or wrinkle, sanctified by Christ Himself, not while on the earth, but in the rapture event itself – without blemish by resurrection or change (I Cor. 15:50-53). All this is the Father's work through Christ, who is, as the Son, the resurrection and the life.

In Christ, the Father has blessed us with many indescribable blessings. We have every spiritual blessing in heavenly places. We are seated in Christ in the heavens – the heavenly seat of the Father's governmental power and glory. We have been promised an inheritance with Christ of all things, visible and invisible. He will share with us all His glory. Yet it remains that the impression on us of these things should not rival in value the Father and the Son's love, desire, and affection for us. Christ loves the church and has given Himself to death for her (Eph. 5:25). The Father loves every adopted son as He does His only Begotten. It is the knowledge of these truths and this relationship from which our desires and affections are generated for the Son and our Father. The inheritance, the glory, the reigning with Him – all cannot touch our proper desire to be with Jesus, and to be in the presence of our Father. Nothing, simply nothing, compares to this.

Chapter 10: Endnotes

[29] In the gospel of John there seems to be a consistent pairing by the Holy Spirit of the terms/names of the Father with the Son – the Son of God, Jesus Christ. Almost every time that Jesus refers to the Father and if He refers to Himself as well, it usually is as the Son of God. It serves, by the Spirit, to establish the relationship and connection between Father and Son that was His mission as the Son to present.

John 5:23

"...that all should honor the Son just as they honor the Father. He who does not honor the Son does not honor the Father who sent Him."

We see the obvious connection between the two names. This same pattern runs throughout the gospel of John. The Son of God was sent to reveal His Father, and this revelation was certainly distinct to believers. It was not for the world and was not for Israel as part of the world. In John 17 we have a beautiful prayer from the Son to the Father that is filled with this pattern indicating the connection between Father and Son.

John 17:1-8

"Jesus spoke these words, lifted up His eyes to heaven, and said: "Father, the hour has come. Glorify Your Son, that Your Son also may glorify You, (2) as You have given Him authority over all flesh, that He should give eternal life to as many as You have given Him. (3) And this is eternal life, that they may know You, the only true God, and Jesus Christ whom You have sent. (4) I have glorified You on the earth. I have finished the work which You have given Me to do. (5) And now, O Father, glorify Me together with Yourself, with the glory which I had with You before the world was."

(6) "I have manifested Your name to the men whom You have given Me out of the world. They were Yours, You gave them to Me, and they have kept Your word. (7) Now they have known that all things which You have given Me are from You. (8) For I have given to them the words which You have given Me; and they have received them, and have known surely that I came forth from You; and they have believed that You sent Me."

<u>Three things to notice</u>: First, it is the Son who glorifies the Father, and the Father who glorifies the Son. It is not at all the same as what you find in John 13:31-32. There we find a different pairing – the title of the Son of Man whose death and shed blood propitiates and glorifies God. Second, the work He refers to as having already finished is the mission of the Son to reveal the Father. This He did by the words, the works, and the will of the Father only. It was a perfect work by the Son glorifying the Father on the earth. Third, the revelation of the Father was specifically directed to the men that the Father had given the Son out of the world. It is a specific revelation to the believer, the other sons.

John 8:28

"Then Jesus said to them, "When you lift up the Son of Man, then you will know that I am He, and that I do nothing of Myself; but as My Father taught Me, I speak these things."

This is an interesting passage. When the Son of Man is lifted up, it is with His death in mind. When this occurs, they would know that He is 'I am', the Son of God. It is the Son of God who does nothing of Himself, but as He is taught by the Father.

Notes

Chapter 11:

His Coming or His Appearing?

n this chapter we will compare and contrast two future events of great Biblical importance. The first is the coming of the Lord for the church, and its departure physically from this world. As you are aware, this is known as the rapture of the church. We have discussed this event in great detail in the previous chapters of this book. The teaching with all the scriptural support presented serves to connect a distinct character, nature, and privilege to this event. I will do my best not to repeat this teaching, but to use it to highlight the distinctions between the two events that their different character and nature present.

The second event is the appearing of Jesus Christ, and this, His manifestation as the Son of Man to the world. This event, we will see, has a completely different character and nature associated with it from Scripture. He is manifested to the world for the judgment of the world. *This defines the character of the event*, and when it occurs it will all proceed according to written prophecy. These general statements already bring out contrasts that distinguish these two events apart from each other.

The Rapture is Christ's coming to retrieve the Church

1 Corinthians 15:23

"But each one in his own order: Christ the firstfruits, afterward those who are Christ's at His coming."

This is speaking of the resurrection of all those who are asleep in Christ at 'His coming' for the church. Those 'in Christ' who are alive at the time will not be excluded. For them it is change, not resurrection. But for both, the alive and the dead in Christ, the accomplishment is the same – the glorifying of the physical body.

2 Thessalonians 2:1

"Now, brethren, concerning the coming of our Lord Jesus Christ and our gathering together to Him, we ask you,"

Again, it is the coming of the Lord. But here we see a little more description. The church is being gathered together to Him. This verse in this second epistle to the Thessalonians is referring back to a passage found in Paul's first epistle to them – that detailed description of the rapture of the church (I Thess. 4:13-18). In that particular passage the event is referred to again as the coming of the Lord (I Thess. 4:15). If we turn to I Thessalonians we may notice how the coming of the Lord Jesus Christ for the saints is presented as common doctrine for the church at the end of every chapter.

1 Thessalonians 1:9-10

"For they themselves declare concerning us what manner of entry we had to you, and how you turned to God from idols to serve the living and true God, (10) and to wait for His Son from heaven, whom He raised from the dead, even Jesus who delivers us from the wrath to come."

1 Thessalonians 2:19

"For what is our hope, or joy, or crown of rejoicing? Is it not even you in the presence of our Lord Jesus Christ at His coming?"

1 Thessalonians 3:13

"...so that He may establish your hearts blameless in holiness before our God and Father at the coming of our Lord Jesus Christ with all His saints."

1 Thessalonians 4:15

"For this we say to you by the word of the Lord, that we who are alive and remain until the coming of the Lord will by no means precede those who are asleep."

1 Thessalonians 5:23

"Now may the God of peace Himself sanctify you completely; and may your whole spirit, soul, and body be preserved blameless at the coming of our Lord Jesus Christ."

The coming of the Lord is for the church, so that He may take His body into the heavens, and into the presence of His Father. Our calling is heavenly. Our citizenship is in the heavens. It is from heaven that we look and wait for the Lord Jesus Christ. When He comes for us He will transform our lowly bodies as conformed to His glorious body, by the exceeding great power of Almighty God (Phil. 3:20-21).

The Lord's Appearing to the World – the Day of Jehovah

The other event is His appearing or manifestation. It is also known in prophecy as the Day of the Lord, even the great and terrible Day of the Lord.

2 Thessalonians 2:2-3

"...not to be soon shaken in mind or troubled, either by spirit or by word or by letter, as if from us, as though the day of Christ had come. (3) Let no one deceive you by any means; for that Day will not come unless the falling away comes first, and the man of sin is revealed, the son of perdition,"

Joel 2:11

"The Lord gives voice before His army,
For His camp is very great;
For strong is the One who executes His word.
For the day of the Lord is great and very terrible;
Who can endure it?"

Isaiah 2:12

"For the day of the Lord of hosts shall come upon everything proud and lofty, upon everything lifted up— and it shall be brought low—"

Isaiah 13:6

"Wail, for the day of the Lord is at hand! It will come as destruction from the Almighty."

Isaiah 13:9

"Behold, the day of the Lord comes, Cruel, with both wrath and fierce anger, to lay the land desolate; And He will destroy its sinners from it."

Joel 1:15

"Alas for the day! For the day of the Lord is at hand; It shall come as destruction from the Almighty."

Joel 2:31

"The sun shall be turned into darkness, And the moon into blood, Before the coming of the great and awesome day of the Lord."

Jeremiah 46:10

"For this is the day of the Lord God of hosts, a day of vengeance, that He may avenge Himself on His adversaries. The sword

shall devour; it shall be satiated and made drunk with their blood; For the Lord God of hosts has a sacrifice in the north country by the River Euphrates."

Amos 5:16

"Therefore the Lord God of hosts, the Lord, says this: "There shall be wailing in all streets, and they shall say in all the highways, 'Alas! Alas!' They shall call the farmer to mourning, And skillful lamenters to wailing."

Amos 5:18

"Woe to you who desire the day of the Lord! For what good is the day of the Lord to you? It will be darkness, and not light."

Zephaniah 1:2

"I will utterly consume everything from the face of the land," Says the Lord;"

Malachi 4:5

"Behold, I will send you Elijah the prophet before the coming of the great and dreadful day of the Lord."

The twelve passages above help to establish the use of the phrase 'the Day of the Lord' and the obvious contrasting character and nature of this event from the descriptions of the rapture of the church. Christ's physical return to this earth is for judgment. It is for the judgment of the world and all things belonging to it. It is an awful and terrible day of destruction and vengeance. It is for the death and condemnation of the prophetic world at that future time.

A Thief in the Night

There is another common phrase found in Scripture that also refers to the Lord's appearing to the world for judgment – *'comes as a thief in the night.'* This phrase is only ever directed to the unbelieving world or that part of professing Christianity left behind that the Lord will treat as the unbelieving world. If we hold this understanding it does clear up for us the meaning of certain passages. For example:

1 Thessalonians 5:2-5

"For you yourselves know perfectly that the day of the Lord so comes as a thief in the night. (3) For when they say, "Peace and safety!" then sudden destruction comes upon them, as labor pains upon a pregnant woman. And they shall not escape. (4) But you, brethren, are not in darkness, so that this Day should overtake you as a thief. (5) You are all sons of light and sons of the day. We are not of the night or of darkness."

Here we easily see that the phrase concerning the thief is paired with of the Day of Jehovah. It is descriptive of how Christ comes suddenly upon a world in darkness, bringing sudden destruction upon them. But the truth of the passage is that it is only for the darkness and His judgment of it. The believer is light in the Lord and of the light of day. Our only association with the Day of the Lord is that we are manifested to the world with Him in glory according to Colossians 3:4. How the church gets in glory beforehand is what Paul just reviewed for the Thessalonians in the previous passage (I Thess. 4:13-18). Again I remind you that the believer being of the light or of the day is our position 'in Christ,' and not based on human effort or an Arminian thought. Christ appears to judge the darkness of the world. His coming as a thief has this attitude and thought.

Revelation 3:3

"Remember therefore how you have received and heard; hold fast and repent. Therefore if you will not watch, I will come upon you as a thief, and you will not know what hour I will come upon you."

This was spoken as a threat by the Lord to the Sardis church. In the progressive history of professing Christianity Sardis represents Protestantism in responsibility after the Reformation. Although it had a great reputation in the eyes of the world, Jesus judges it as to what it actually is – dead. He will treat it just like the world.

Luke 17:26-30

"And as it was in the days of Noah, so it will be also in the days of the Son of Man: (27) They ate, they drank, they married wives, they were given in marriage, until the day that Noah entered the ark, and the flood came and destroyed them all. (28) Likewise as it was also in the days of Lot: They ate, they drank, they bought, they sold, they planted, they built; (29) but on the day that Lot went out of Sodom it rained fire and brimstone from heaven and destroyed them all. (30) Even so will it be in the day when the Son of Man is revealed."

This is the world, including most of Israel, at the time when the Son of Man is manifested. It is the world truly saying, "Peace and safety!" It is business as usual. It is being oblivious to the approaching events. It is as a thief coming in the night.

The Warring Judgment of the Son of Man

Revelation 19:17-21

"Then I saw an angel standing in the sun; and he cried with a loud voice, saying to all the birds that fly in the midst of heaven, "Come and gather together for the supper of the great God, (18) that you may eat the flesh of kings, the flesh of captains, the flesh of mighty men, the flesh of horses and of those who sit on them, and the flesh of all people, free and slave, both small and great."

(19) "And I saw the beast, the kings of the earth, and their armies, gathered together to make war against Him who sat on the horse and against His army. (20) Then the beast was captured, and with him the false prophet who worked signs in his presence, by which he deceived those who received the mark of the beast and those who worshiped his image. These two were cast alive into the lake of fire burning with brimstone. (21) And the rest were killed with the sword which

proceeded from the mouth of Him who sat on the horse. And all the birds were filled with their flesh."

This is what will happen on the earth when the KING OF KINGS AND LORD OF LORDS returns. He has a sharp sword out of His mouth by which He strikes the nations and rules them with a rod of iron. He will cast into the lake of fire the two beasts – the full symbolic representation of a rebellious, blasphemous, and apostate world – and their heads, the Caesar and the Antichrist. Christ's garments will be dipped in the blood of His enemies (Is. 63:1-6). He will utterly consume and destroy. It is the great wrath and fierce anger of the Lord, a time of darkness and wailing.

The Differing Character of the Two Events

Does all this sound anything like the rapture of the church? Does any of it sound like the uplifting passage in I Thess. 4:13-18, where the dead in Christ rise first, and we who remain are caught up together with them, so that we may ever be with the Lord? Do any of the above passages that speak of the day of the Lord end with this phrase, "…therefore comfort one another with these words?" (I Thess. 4:18) When the Lord promised in John 14 He would return for us, He prefaced it by saying, "Let not your heart be troubled." However, all of the above quoted passages concerning His appearing to the world are intended to be troubling and discomforting! That is the character and nature of the Day of the Lord, and it stands in great contrast from what describes His coming for the church.

2 Timothy 4:1

"I charge you therefore before God and the Lord Jesus Christ, who will judge the living and the dead at His appearing and His kingdom:"

The Judicial Judgments of the Son of Man

His appearing is to the world. It is the Son of Man returning in great glory to sit on His throne of glory. He will judge the living at that time, at the time of His appearing. It will be the separating of the sheep from the goats of the remaining Gentile nations (Matt. 25:31-33). His kingdom is the kingdom of the Son of Man, which during the millennium, grows up in glory to fill the entire earth (Dan. 2:34-35, 44-45). At the end of this period the Son of Man judges the dead at the great white throne (John 5:22, 27, Rev. 20:11-15).

Colossians 3:1-4

"If then you were raised with Christ, seek those things which are above, where Christ is, sitting at the right hand of God. (2) Set your mind on things above, not on things on the earth. (3) For you died, and your life is hidden with Christ in God. (4) When Christ who is our life appears, then you also will appear with Him in glory."

Again, His appearing is to the world. At this present time Christ is hidden in God, hidden from the world (v. 3). This is the contrast set up in this passage – hidden from the world verses being manifested to the eyes of the world. But Christ is never hidden from the eye of faith. More so, our life is Christ, and is hidden in God from the world like Him. However, both Christ and the church appear together – manifested to the world. In order for this to occur, the church would have to already be in glory with Him, having already been taken there.

The Church appears to the World in Glory with Him

The rapture of the church places us in the heavenly glory according to the heavenly calling we possess (Heb. 3:1). The first three verses of the above passage are pointing to this calling. We have this by virtue of 'having died' and being 'raised with Christ.' Christ has already entered into the heavenly glory. It simply remains for His body to join Him there. That is why our life is hidden there – this life we possess has nothing to do with this world, they do not see or understand it. The life is Christ, and Christ is sitting and hidden at the right hand of God. However, this very life, in the rapture, is what swallows up mortality (II Cor. 5:4). For the dead in Christ, in the rapture, this life is what swallows up the corruption of the grave (I Cor. 15:52-53).

It should be clear that in order for the church to appear with Christ when He appears to the world, we would have to already be with Him when He returns to the earth. The emphasis of the verse (v. 4) is the word 'appear.' It is used twice: first for Christ appearing to the world, the second for the church. The emphasis is not the glory – it is just that when the world sees the church with Christ at His appearing, the appearing itself is associated with glory. Jesus is already in the glory. When the church appears to the world it will already have been glorified.

There are two other passages I want to share that are directly connected with the thought of the church with Christ at His appearing.

Romans 8:19-22

"For the earnest expectation of the creation eagerly waits for the revealing of the sons of God. (20) For the creation was subjected to futility, not willingly, but because of Him who subjected it in hope; (21) because the creation itself also will be delivered from the bondage of corruption into the glorious liberty of the children of God. (22) For we know that the whole creation groans and labors with birth pangs together until now."

When the sons of God appear with Jesus Christ it will be the time when creation will be delivered from its own corruption. The appearing of the sons of God with Christ in glory is how the sons are 'revealed' to this present creation. This specific revelation to creation is for its deliverance.

John 17:22-24

"And the glory which You gave Me I have given them, that they may be one just as We are one: (23) I in them, and You in Me; that they may be made perfect in one, and that the world may know that You have sent Me, and have loved them as You have loved Me."

(24) *"Father, I desire that they also whom You gave Me may be with Me where I am, that they may behold My glory which You have given Me; for You loved Me before the foundation of the world."*

The Father's love for the Believer

Jesus Christ shares His glory with all the other sons of God. He also has a fervent desire for all those given to Him from the Father to be with Him in the Father's presence – all the sons together in the Fathers house. We will go there and be in the glory with Him according to His previous promise in John 14:1-3 – the rapture. However, we know that we will be with Christ when He appears to the world. This is when the world will know. Know what? When the world sees the church with Christ in glory, they will know beyond any doubt that Christ is of God and always has been, and that the Father loves the church as He loves the Son. It does not say the world will believe, but that the world will know, because they will see with their own eyes the church in the glory of God.[30]

Having shown you the differing character and nature of the two events, we turn to listing some further differences in order to clearly see that they are, in fact, distinct events.

The Rapture is part of the hidden Mystery – always

1.) The rapture of the church is part of the mystery given to Paul to reveal. This mystery is the existence of the body of Christ and all its doctrine. This stewardship was personally given to Paul (Eph. 3:2-4, 7-8, Col.1:25). The rapture is the revelation of how the mystery on the earth ends – the church in mass departing this world. Only Paul teaches the doctrine of the church.[31] Only Paul laid the foundation for the building of the church on the earth, a foundation no other was given the responsibility for (I Cor. 3:9-11). Only Paul teaches the rapture as related to church doctrine.[32] All aspects of the mystery are completely hidden from the prophets (Eph. 3:5, 9, Col.

1:26). The mystery includes the heavenly calling of the body of Christ. The mystery is never the proper subject of Biblical prophecy.

The Day of the Lord – the appearing of Christ – is very much the subject of prophecy. That is why you will find it referenced all over the Old Testament and in the book of Revelation. As part of prophecy it points to God's government of the earth, and heavily involves the nation of Israel. The earthly calling is Israel, which is the proper subject of biblical prophecy.

Heavenly and Earthly Things

2.) The Day of the Lord is primarily about saving a Jewish remnant on the earth, and the ensuing building of a nation by God from what He sovereignly saves. The return of Christ to the earth is the second coming of the Jewish Messiah to Israel (Matt. 23:39). The return of Christ to the earth is God dealing with His earthly calling. The true church will not be here. *God will not be dealing with two distinct callings at the same time.*

The rapture is about the heavenly calling, the removal of the body of Christ into the heavens from the earth. The church is the heavenly calling (Heb. 3:1), and is the heavenly glory of Jesus Christ in the counsels of God. Our citizenship is in heaven (Phil. 3:20). We are seated in heavenly places in Christ and blessed with all spiritual blessing in the heavens (Eph. 1:3, 2:6). The calling of the church reveals God's purpose for it. The calling of the church is its destiny, and it is not on the earth. The Son of Man glorified has already entered into the heavens. Now the Spirit has been sent to the earth to gather His body, the church. Christ will not take up His power and reign, nor receive His inheritance, without being joined to His body. God will take all believers in Christ into the heavens according to our calling. This is the establishing of the heavenly glory of Christ, to the eternal glory of God.

God is not dealing with the earthly calling at the present time – it has been set aside. Israel has been set aside as seen in Hosea 1:9, 'you are not My people.' This was physically demonstrated by judgment in 70 AD with the destruction of Jerusalem and its temple. God is not sealing and preserving an earthly remnant in Israel yet, with a physical seal on their foreheads (Rev. 7:3). However, God is currently sealing the heavenly calling. This seal of authenticity is the placement of His Spirit in the believer (Eph. 1:13). The presence of this seal is all the difference in the glorifying of the church at the rapture event – *"But if the Spirit of Him who raised Jesus from the dead dwells in you, He who raised Christ from the dead will also give life to your mortal bodies through His Spirit who dwells in you."* (Rom. 8:11) The seal of the Spirit distinguishes those who will be involved in the rapture. It distinguishes the true church in the crop of professing Christianity (Matt. 13:24-26, 38).

The Rapture is not an Appearing to this World

3.) The coming of the Lord for the church is a catching up of all believers into the clouds to meet the Lord in the air (I Thess. 4:17). This could not be any clearer. The Lord does not even touch the earth at this time. He takes us to our Father. It is not a U-turn in the air. The rapture is part of the mystery of the doctrine of the church. But its physical occurrence is mystery as well – it will not be an open manifestation to the world at all. I doubt the world will realize the true church is gone. If they sense anything missing they will make their excuses for it and go their way. For the world it will not be of much consequence because they are *the dwellers of the earth* (Rev. 1:7, 3:10, 6:11, 8:13, 11:10, 12:12, 13:8, 14, 14:6, 17:2, and 8).[33]

The Day of the Lord is the physical return of Jesus Christ to the earth. His feet will stand on the Mount of Olives outside Jerusalem, and the mount will split from east to west (Zech. 14:4). The catching up is for the heavens. His appearing to the world is for the earth.

The Rapture – no signs. The Day of the Lord – with signs and wonders

4.) The believer/church has a walk of faith while on this earth. After the rapture, when we are in the glory of God, we will no longer be on a walk, but will have entered the rest of God. We will have no need of faith, because all our hopes will be seen and realized (Rom. 8:24-25). There are no prophetic events standing between the present time and the catching up of the church. That is why the coming of the Lord is a constant present expectation of the true church. The only scriptural idea that remains is 'the fullness of the Gentiles' coming into the church, and that quantity only the Father knows (Rom. 11:25). When that fullness occurs, the church will be taken – no signs, no warnings, no earthly events needed to precede the church's conclusion on the earth.

The appearing of Christ to the world is accompanied by signs and certain preceding prophetic events.[34] The appearing itself is a sign – *"Then the sign of the Son of Man will appear in heaven, and then all the tribes of the earth will mourn, and they will see the Son of Man coming on the clouds of heaven with power and great glory."* (Matt. 24:30) The Day of the Lord is for judgment. The prophetic objects of the worldly evil must have fully developed and be present around Jerusalem for the prophecies to be fulfilled (Rev. 13). Israel as a nation is always saved and delivered through judgment. Noah and Lot serve as types in this biblical principle, while the plagues of Egypt and the parting of the Red Sea serve as the physical evidence of the principle at Israel's inception. At Christ's appearing,

Israel will be delivered as a Jewish remnant, preserved in the midst of the judgments.[35]

Israel is connected to the earth by their religion and promises. Judaism is a walk by sight and senses. That is why 'the Jews request a sign.' (I Cor. 1:22, Matt. 12:38-39, 16:1, Mark 8:11-12, Luke 11:16, 29) The disciple Thomas is a type prefiguring the Jewish remnant in the end – they will not believe in Jesus Christ as Messiah without seeing first. "They will look on Me whom they have pierced." (Zech. 12:10) A walk by sight, senses, and signs is the character of the things of the earth. Judaism is God's given religion for the earth, and Israel is God's earthly calling. The appearing of Christ is also for delivering a sealed, saved, and preserved Jewish remnant. God's purpose in His counsels in this is obvious – by His faithfulness to fulfill all His promises, He builds a nation that His government of the earth is centralized in. This will be the real Israel. It will be solely the work of God. And as the work of God it will not fail.

The Lord's appearing to the world in the end will be the full establishment of divine power in God's government of the earth. Contrary to this, the rapture of the church and its entrance into the Father's house is the accomplishment of sovereign grace towards the believer/church. It is the end or consummation of our salvation and the entrance of the church into the rest of God. His appearing to the world is not for rest, but rather for vengeance through righteous judgment.

The idea of keeping the Body of Christ on the earth waiting for Christ to return and judge the world is the denial of the church's proper hopes and proper relationship with Christ. It is the mixing and the confounding of two distinct callings – that of Israel and that of the church. By default it is the Judaizing of Christian teaching. It is the reduction of Christian hopes to their lowest possible level, while still allowing them to be associated in any way with being saved – on the earth waiting with the world. The denial is false teaching and the devil's mischief. Jesus promised, *"I will come again and receive you to Myself; that where I am, there you may be also."* This is the true hope of the church.

Chapter 11: Endnotes

[30] Just previous to this verse in John 17 Jesus uses the phrase 'that the world may believe that You sent Me.' This is speaking of believers in our walk on the earth being in unity with Christ and one another, and our communion with the Father and the Son while here. When the world sees this unity and communion, they will believe that Christ was sent by God (John 17:20-21). However, in vs. 22-23, He speaks of believers in glory being made perfect in one. When the world sees this at His appearing, the church with Him in glory, they will know that the Father loves the believer as He does His Son. The world will know because they will see it with their own eyes – the church in glory.

[31] If you examine the writings of the other epistle writers, you will not find any teaching or doctrine about the body of Christ. God used Paul only to reveal it. It was his responsibility, his stewardship, to reveal the church. Paul's conversion experience centers on the revelation of the church. Jesus says to him, "Saul, Saul, why are you persecuting Me?" The Lord and His body are one. To persecute the church is to persecute Jesus. The revelation of the mystery – the body of Christ – is part of Paul from the moment of his conversion.

There is another important distinction in Paul's conversion experience to consider, one that makes him different than the other apostles. Of all the apostles, Paul alone sees Jesus Christ in glory. The testimony of any apostle is of what they are eye-witnesses of. The testimony of the twelve is all about what they saw, and heard, and touched (I John 1:1-3, II Pet. 1:16-18, John 15:27). The testimony of the twelve is of Christ's walk in the flesh, His resurrection from the dead, and them losing sight of Him in the clouds at His ascension (Acts 1:9). The character of the testimony of the twelve is well depicted in Peter's words when he was brought by the Spirit to Cornelius' house.

Acts 10:36-41

"The word which God sent to the children of Israel, preaching peace through Jesus Christ—He is Lord of all— (37) that word you know, which was proclaimed throughout all Judea, and began from Galilee after the baptism which John preached: (38) how God anointed Jesus of Nazareth with the Holy Spirit and with power, who went about doing good and healing all who were oppressed by the devil, for

God was with Him. (39) And we are witnesses of all things which He did both in the land of the Jews and in Jerusalem, whom they killed by hanging on a tree. (40) Him God raised up on the third day, and showed Him openly, (41) not to all the people, but to witnesses chosen before by God, even to us who ate and drank with Him after He arose from the dead."

The twelve, among whom Peter was most prominent, testified of a Christ walking with them, and a Christ who they ate with after He was raised from the dead. It is the simple testimony of their experiences. But this is the difference to be recognized in Paul and what makes him such a different apostle from the twelve. Paul sees Christ in heavenly glory. His testimony is only of a Christ in glory. He does not know a Christ after the flesh, like the twelve (II Cor. 5:16). Not only that, but he teaches, *"Even though we have known Christ according to the flesh, yet now we know Him thus no longer."* He teaches that all believers can only now know a Christ in glory. And further, being united by the Spirit to a Christ in glory, from now on we are not to regard each other according to the flesh. Paul's doctrine of the church is its formation and gathering by the Spirit sent down, and the unity of this body to the Head exalted in glory. This unity to Christ is by the baptism of the same Spirit (I Cor. 12:12-14).

Paul's doctrine of the church is always in reference to a Christ exalted far above the heavens, and a body united to Him in glory (Eph. 1:20-23, 4:8-12). This is the body of Christ, this is the true church. It is not a uniting to a Christ in the flesh, nor a testimony of a Christ in the flesh. This is not a Jewish testimony according to what eye-witnesses saw, and heard, and touched in the flesh. It is not the testimony of the twelve to Israel, still hoping for the nation's repentance so that Jesus would quickly return from heaven as their Messiah and set up the Messianic kingdom (Acts 3:13-21). Paul's doctrine is not the testimony of the apostles of the circumcision (Gal. 2:7-8). Paul's gospel is the gospel of the glory of Jesus Christ (II Cor. 4:4, II Thess. 2:14). It wasn't passed on to him by man, nor from Peter or the other eleven, but directly from Jesus Christ Himself (Gal. 1:11-12).

Jesus mentions the church twice (Matt. 16:18, 18:17), but only in passing, and never to teach doctrine concerning it. When Jesus says, "...I will build My church..." there are two important points made.

- First, His words are future tense – I will build. The church did not exist at that time. It would not exist until after He was glorified and the Holy Spirit sent down at Pentecost.

Many teachers and scholars say the assembly of Israel in the wilderness is the church simply because the same word "assembly" is used. This same word is used to describe the mob that gathered to stone Paul outside one of the cities he went to in the book of Acts. We would not mistake this mob as a reference to the church and neither should we see Israel as the actual church passing through the Red Sea and delivered out of slavery in Egypt. What we should see and properly understand is the specific times and experiences with Israel that serve as a type and shadow, and what specifically the experience typifies. Israel is always an example for instruction to the believer/church in all their ways and experiences. This statement does not mean that every experience Israel had typified the believer/church, or for that matter professing Christendom. Every type and shadow is in general an example, but every example is not specifically a type and shadow.

Israel's history and experiences serve as types for three different entities – professing Christendom, the true believer/church, and finally a Jewish remnant saved and restored in the land during the millennium. They typify Christendom (a spoiled crop of wheat and tares mixed together) from their deliverance out of Egypt through all their wonderings in the wilderness. They typify the body of Christ in their crossing of Jordan and being circumcised under Joshua – the rapture of the church and the glorifying of our bodies upon entrance into the rest of God (glory). Once in the land from the battle of Jericho on, including King David, and Solomon, the son of David sitting on Jehovah's throne, Israel serves as a type of how a Jewish remnant will be saved and delivered and restored in the Promised Land in the end. Israel serves as these types in that order in time. The substance of the types appears in that order in time as well.

Is Israel in the wilderness actually the church? I would ask, does Israel in the wilderness even typify the church? When you keep in mind that the church is actually the body of Christ, a body united to the Head glorified to the right hand of God, far above all principalities and power and might and dominion (Eph. 1:19-23), and it is the workmanship of God (Eph. 2:10), then you confidently answer 'no' to both questions. Tares exist and are present – the planting of Satan – in the spoiled crop of Christendom in the field of the world. There are no tares in the body of Christ. Yet there were tares in the assembly of Israel in the wilderness. The tares among them all fell in the wilderness in judgment, God swearing He would not allow them to enter the land (Heb. 3:16-19). How can Israel in the wilderness be the church? I would say in the wilderness Israel does not even typify the church.

Jesus will build His church. The Lord's words were future tense. I believe the church began on the day of Pentecost. Each member had God dwelling in them as the sons of God, sealed by the Spirit. This is the Spirit of adoption of sonship, the deposit and guarantee of glory. The difference is that God's seal of authenticity is dwelling in them, the Holy Spirit abiding in the believer forever (John 14:16-17). It is this same Holy Spirit sent down from above that forms the body, the church (I Cor. 12:12-13).

• Second, His words speak of a sovereign work of His alone, and not of man. Man does not do this. What Jesus builds is not given to man to build on the earth. All believers are God's workmanship, created in Christ. God's workmanship cannot fail. We are all predestined, all chosen, all called, and all justified by the work of God (Rom. 8:29-30). And God will glorify all the sons – conforming them to the image of His Son – by the rapture of the church. We have to realize that the entire listing in Romans 8 is all the sovereign work of God and will not fail.

What can fail and does fail is what man builds on the earth that is called the professing church. Paul laid the foundation for this building that no other could lay. But men (ministers) must take heed how they build. This is on the earth and involves human responsibility (I Cor. 3:5-17). The history of man given responsibility is well documented in Scripture.

[32] Paul alone ties the rapture event to the mystery and doctrine of the church (I Cor. 15:51-55). When Jesus speaks of the rapture, there is no corporate entity in mind (John 14:1-3). His promise is to individual believers who are chosen out of the world and made sons of God. But Paul's stewardship was to teach the mystery, the doctrine of the body

of Christ, and to lay a foundation on the earth for the building of a great house (II Tim. 2:19-21). The rapture is included in the mystery of the body – how the church is glorified and ends its time on the earth.

[33] The phrase 'dwellers of the earth' or 'inhabitants of the earth' or something very similar to this is used numerous times in the book of Revelation. It is a prophetic phrase descriptive of what is part of the world and to be judged as the world. The entire book of Revelation is God's judgment of the responsibility of the world – all will be judged by their works (Rev. 20:12-13). A slight deviation of the use of the phrase is presented in the description of the second beast of Revelation 13 – *"Then I saw another beast coming up out of the earth..."* This is the antichrist. He comes up in the end out of what is already firmly established as the prophetic earth. He is of the world and of the earth, as is the nation of Israel in their calling. He will be a false Christ and a false prophet for this deceived nation (Matt. 24:24).

[34] It may be profitable to see more of the events that are between the rapture of the church and the appearing of the Lord to the world, particularly the end and judgment of professing Christianity on the earth. Revelation 19:14 shows us that we come with Him, which is after the officiating of the marriage of the church to Christ in heaven (Rev. 19:7-9, Eph. 5:25-27), which is after the destruction and judgment of the false bride with earthly glory on the earth (Rev. 17:1-18). The false bride judged is the tares bundled together and left in the field of the world. Her judgment comes after the wheat is removed from out of her and out of the world (Matt. 13:30). The harlot is professing Christianity, the spoiled crop in the field.

This is the Biblical principle found in Revelations 17-19 that is so important for spiritual clarity – God judges the false bride of the Lamb and destroys her on the earth *before* the true bride of the Lamb is celebrated in heaven. The great Babylonian harlot pretends to be the bride of the Lamb on the earth, adorned with earthly riches, luxury, and glory, and filled with abominations (idolatry) and the filthiness of her fornications (Rev. 17:4-5). It is with the kings of the earth that she committed her fornications (Rev. 17:2). It is called her fornications because she *should have been* in relationship with someone else. Who? – With the Lamb, the Son of God. Instead, she is having relationship with the world and the kings of the earth. The inhabitants of the earth are intoxicated with her earthly agenda and they lose all spiritual insight and direction. The great harlot pretends to be the bride of Christ.

To carry on her pretention she would have to have a Christian profession. She would have to profess Jesus Christ. This great harlot cannot possibly be Islam, as is being brokered today in some circles of Christian teaching as the new and correct understanding of this particular prophetic element. Islam has always rejected Jesus Christ as the Son of God, and certainly as the Lamb of God slain to take away the sins of the world. In principle, Islam does not fulfill this position or prophetic allegory. This should be obvious to all spiritually minded believers. What professes Jesus Christ is not Islam. It is not Judaism. It is professing Christendom.

This false earthly bride of Christ is judged before the end. The end is a generalized term for when Christ returns to the earth to bind Satan and cast the two beasts into the lake of fire. He then establishes the kingdom of the Son of Man, which eventually fills the whole earth – not truly an end to anything per se, except the end of Gentile dominion in civil world government. Judgment begins at the house of God and the false bride, the tares of professing Christianity, will be judged before the world is judged (Matt. 13:40). God uses the ten kings to destroy the whore (Rev. 17:16), casting her influence off the Roman beast, allowing the Roman beast to then ascend out of the bottomless pit in its final form (Rev. 17:8). The harlot cast off the beast occurs before the end.

The great harlot of Rev. 17 should be an interesting understanding for all believers, as it was for John. When he sees it sitting on the beast and realizes what she represents, he 'marvels with great amazement.' (vs. 3-6). She is the professing Christian church world. In general, her influence has been over the Gentile nations of the world – she sits on many waters (v. 1). Her harlotry has been particularly with the kings of the prophetic earth (v. 2) – this would be the land masses and the Gentile nations included in the boundaries of the four Gentile world monarchies (Dan. 7), the four beasts. In the vision John sees her sitting on the 4th beast, the Roman Empire (v. 3). What exactly does this mean?

There are three distinct states revealed concerning our understanding of the 4th beast (v. 8). *"The beast that you saw was, and is not, and will ascend out of the bottomless pit and go to perdition."* The key to the passage is not specifically thinking of 'time' or 'existence of the beast,' but instead, the character and nature of a beast being displayed – apostasy, rebellion, blasphemy, and independence from God. In John's time, which also includes the time of Christ in the flesh, the beast 'was' – it existed as a beast, the evil and apostate Roman Empire. This is depicted by the two legs of iron in the statue in the king's dream (Dan. 2:33, 40). This is the first state of the 4th beast.

If we skip to the third state of the 4th beast, it is the one in which it will ascend out of the bottomless pit. This is its worse form and final state. This is the time when Satan is cast down to the earth, and he gives the Roman beast and it's Caesar his authority, power, and throne (Rev. 13:2). This is depicted by the feet and toes of iron and clay in the statue (Dan. 2:33-35, 41-43). This third state of the 4th beast 'coming to character again' out of the bottomless pit is also depicted in Rev. 13:1-6, in the time of the last three and a half years, sometime after the dragon is kicked out of the heavens (Rev. 12:7-9), Satan knowing his time is short (Rev. 12:12 – the short time is the three and a half years). We know this is its last form, not only because it was given authority to continue for forty-two months (Rev. 13:5), but also because the ten horns have crowns (Rev. 13:1). These are the ten kings who give their power to the last Caesar, the head of the final form of this Roman beast (Dan. 7:8, 24).

In John's vision of the woman sitting on the beast (Rev. 17), the ten horns do not have crowns yet (Rev. 17:3, 7, 12). This is the second state of the 4th beast. This state is referred to by the angel as 'and is not' (Rev. 17:8), and is the state of the beast that the *vision* deals with. It is the state of the beast when it loses its character as a beast. The second state of the 4th beast is all the time when the woman is sitting on the beast. She is professing Christianity and she has Christianized the Roman beast. During this time the beast does not act in the 'character' of a beast – it simply 'is not.' This time began when the Roman Empire was declared a 'Christian Empire' under Constantine. The beast was no longer acting in the 'character' of a beast, but now professed Jesus Christ. This second state of the beast with the harlot sitting on it continues to this present day.

But it is also clear that the third and final form of the 4th beast is anti-Christian. There is no woman riding the beast in Revelation 13. It is a fully apostate and blasphemous form, with a will of its own, and entirely anti-Christian (Rev. 13:6). The ten horns are used of God to cast off the woman, and this, at some point before they come to power and have their crowns (Rev. 17:16-17). The ten horns hate the harlot and her influence. She is judged and destroyed, her influence ended over the beast. This brings an end to the second state of the 4th beast – the state where it 'is not.' The harlot has to be cast off the beast before the beast can resume its character as a beast. Always remember – the vision of the beast in Revelation 17 precedes the vision of the beast in Revelation 13.

[35] Noah and Lot serve as types of how, as a Jewish remnant, Israel is saved in the end. They are purged and saved, refined if you will, through judgment. This type is easily perceived in the Lord's own prophetic statements. *Luke 17:26-30*

"And as it was in the days of Noah, so it will be also in the days of the Son of Man: They ate, they drank, they married wives, they were given in marriage, until the day that Noah entered the ark, and the flood came and destroyed them all. Likewise as it was also in the days of Lot: They ate, they drank, they bought, they sold, they planted, they built; but on the day that Lot went out of Sodom it rained fire and brimstone from heaven and destroyed them all. Even so will it be in the day when the Son of Man is revealed."

Notes

Chapter 12:

The Coming Tribulation.

aving established in the previous chapter the differences in Scripture between Christ's appearing to the world (the Day of the Lord) and His coming for the church (the rapture), we will move on to say a few things concerning the timing of the event. For many believers this is the issue – when? Believers do not question whether I Thessalonians 4:13-18 is inspired Scripture. None of us would say it isn't. And so the passage must be explained. This is where we like to argue about the timing of the event. What we must realize in this discussion is that our mistakes and misunderstandings serve to rob all significance and privilege associated with the church in the event itself.

Having read this far in the book, the reader should be fairly clear on the timing already. In the previous chapter, when Christ appears to the world, the church appears with Him in His glory (Col. 3:4). The only plausible explanation is that the church is already with Him in the glory of God in order to appear with Him to the world.

There is coming a period of time on the earth of great trouble and turmoil. It will be a time of the greatest manifestations of evil and corruption. It will be unprecedented hardship and suffering. And it will be a time when the judgment and wrath of God will be poured out on an unbelieving world. We refer to this period of time as the coming tribulation. The world around the believer is simply ripening to this time. The Scriptures speak of a period of tribulation. If we pay close attention we will understand the character of this time.

Jeremiah 30:7

"Alas! For that day is great, So that none is like it; And it is the time of Jacob's trouble, But he shall be saved out of it."

Daniel 12:1

"At that time Michael shall stand up,
The great prince who stands watch over the sons of your people;
And there shall be a time of trouble,
Such as never was since there was a nation,
Even to that time.
And at that time your people shall be delivered,
Everyone who is found written in the book."

Matthew 24:21-22

"For then there will be great tribulation, such as has not been since the beginning of the world until this time, no, nor ever shall be. And unless those days were shortened, no flesh would be saved; but for the elect's sake those days will be shortened."

The Character of the Coming Tribulation

- First, it is a time of great trouble as the world has never seen before, not since there have been nations formed on the face of the earth. The trouble and devastation is so extreme that if God did not shorten the time of it, all flesh would be lost – physical life. The passage from Matthew 24 tells us the time was shortened for the elect's sake – this is the Jewish remnant in the end.

- Second, it is decidedly a Jewish time of reckoning. It is specifically called Jacob's trouble. For the most part it is about Daniel's people, which is literally Israel. Daniel was in captivity with his people. All the prophecies and visions given to Daniel only concerned the things that would befall his people – the Jews.

- Third, as a people, Israel will be delivered through the trouble. The third passage above, from Matthew 24, uses the word 'tribulation' and identifies how Israel is saved as a nation – an elect Jewish remnant. Matthew 24:2 refers directly to the destruction of Jerusalem and the temple in 70 AD. Much of the rest of Matthew 24 is Jesus referring to the time of Jacob's trouble and He is giving instructions directly to the elect Jewish remnant in the end. This part of Jesus' prophetic statements deal only with Jerusalem, Judea, and the temple. All of Matthew 24 is localized and very Jewish in language and character.[36] There should be no doubt that the events spoken of here all center on Jerusalem and Judea.

Revelation 3:10

"Because you have kept My command to persevere, I also will keep you from the hour of trial which shall come upon the whole world, to test those who dwell on the earth."

The Prophetic Earth – the expansive territories of the Four World Dynasties

In a general way the tribulation will be experienced worldwide. However, there should be no doubt that the concentration of events is in what I call the prophetic earth – the masses of land included in the four Gentile dynasties. The fourth beast of Daniel's vision (Dan. 7:7) was the Roman Empire in the time of Christ. It is this same Roman beast that is resurrected out of the bottomless pit in the period of the tribulation (Rev. 17:8, 13:1-8, 11:7). This beast has the characteristics of the three empires that preceded it (Rev. 13:1-2), but is the perfection of apostate evil (seven heads), that is given Satan's direct authority, power, and throne on the earth.

The True Church is kept out of the Hour of Trial

The passage also shows that the true church will be kept out of this period of tribulation. A better translation would be 'you have kept the word of My patience.' Christ is presently waiting at the right hand of God. He has been waiting from the time He sat down, having accomplished our eternal redemption, till His enemies are made His footstool (Heb. 10:12-14). As believers we enter into His patience by waiting with Him and as He waits. He will not take His inheritance without His fellow-heirs with Him. *The rapture of the body of Christ will occur before the coming hour of testing the entire world – the tribulation.* Philadelphia, to whom these words were addressed, represents the true church in the end (Rev. 3:11-12).

You might object that Thyatira is told she will be thrown into great tribulation (Rev. 2:22), thinking this is the church as well. It is true that Thyatira, as a whole, will still be on the earth during the tribulation and under judgment. But please look at who He is speaking to. Does Thyatira represent the true church? The Lord's words describe her. For the most part she is Jezebel, a false prophetess teaching and beguiling His true servants. Her sexual immorality is her union with the world. Her eating things sacrificed to idols, is the idolatry and abominations she practices. She births her own children in her false doctrines and corruption, teaching the depths of Satan (Rev. 2:20-24). Jesus will cast her into a sickbed of judgment and into the tribulation. Does that sound like something He would do to His own body (Eph. 5:29)? Does this sound like the true wheat, the true church? No, it sounds like the main features and teachings of Roman Catholicism – her pretenses, her superstitions, her worldliness and idolatry.

The Candlesticks – the responsibility of the Spoiled Crop in the Field

In Revelation 2, 3, the Son of Man is judging the candlesticks (Rev. 1:12-13). These candlesticks are not the body of Christ. The candlesticks (the light from the candlestick) represent the responsibility of the spoiled crop of wheat and tares in the field of the world (Matt. 13:24-30, 37-39). The spoiled crop is all of professing Christianity together. If we fail to see the candlestick as the corporate responsibility of the crop, or fail to see the spoiled crop as wheat and tares mixed together, then we will not properly understand the things He is saying and judging.

This vision of the Son of Man walking among the candlesticks is on the earth. John's next vision in Revelation 4 takes him into heaven. The responsibility of man on earth is always subject to judgment from God because it is man's work, it is man building. Here Jesus is judging the responsibility of the church world as a corporate entity, as professing Christianity progresses through time. All the details describing the Son of Man in this vision are details depicting His right to judge the works of man on the earth (Rev. 1:12-16).

Further, God does not and will not judge His own work (this is a Biblical principle worth remembering). The body of Christ is His own workmanship created in Christ, and it was the Son of Man alone who planted the wheat (Matt. 13:37). However, Christ is standing among the candlesticks judging the responsibility of the spoiled crop. The responsibility is the works of man as he has built on the earth (I Cor. 3:9-17). It is the works of all there is that names the name of Jesus Christ corporately.

If we look closely at the parable of the wheat and tares (Matt. 13:24-30) and its interpretation (Matt. 13:37-43) we may learn certain important realities. In the Son of Man's 'time of harvest' the wheat is removed from the field (world) and into His barn (taken to heaven – Matt. 13:30). This is the rapture of the true church – only the wheat being removed from the world. The field is left behind unchanged – this is the world of unbelieving Jews and Gentiles. The spoiled crop of wheat and tares mixed together – professing Christianity – existed for a long time as a separate corporate entity in the field of the world. The judgment of the field is not dealt with in this particular parable. What is dealt with is the judgment of the tares of professing Christianity – they had been bundled together and left behind in the field 'to be burned' at their given time of judgment (Matt. 13:30). This judgment is made certain in the interpretation (Matt. 13:40).

The true church will not be on the earth during the tribulation. When Christ is manifested to the world at the end of the tribulation, His bride will be with Him. For the church to appear in glory with Him, we would have to have been previously glorified. This reality is further established in many other Scriptures. In Revelation 19, John's vision shows more details concerning the great and terrible day of the Lord – again it is Christ's appearing to the world.

The details of the Day of the Lord

Revelation 19:11-18

Now I saw heaven opened, and behold, a white horse. And He who sat on him was called Faithful and True, and in righteousness He judges and makes war. (12) His eyes were like a flame of fire, and on His head were many crowns. He had a name written that no one knew except Himself. (13) He was clothed with a robe dipped in blood, and His name is called The Word of God. (14) And the armies in heaven, clothed in fine linen, white and clean, followed Him on white horses. (15) Now out of His mouth goes a sharp sword, that with it He should strike the nations. And He Himself will rule them with a rod of iron. He Himself treads the winepress of the fierceness and wrath of Almighty God. (16) And He has on His robe and on His thigh a name written:

KING OF KINGS AND
LORD OF LORDS

(17)"Then I saw an angel standing in the sun; and he cried with a loud voice, saying to all the birds that fly in the midst

of heaven, "Come and gather together for the supper of the great God, (18) that you may eat the flesh of kings, the flesh of captains, the flesh of mighty men, the flesh of horses and of those who sit on them, and the flesh of all people, free and slave, both small and great."

This is His appearing in glory to the world, and it is obvious He will be executing judgment on the world as the Son of Man (Rev. 1:7, Matt. 24:30, Dan. 7:13, Mark 14:62). The title 'King of Kings and Lord of Lords' is reference to the Son of Man title. His name being 'The Word of God' is who He was and is eternally – the Son of God (v. 13 above). This depicts Jesus Christ, the Son of God as the Son of Man.

The Armies of Heaven with the Son of Man

This passage shows other realities as well. The appearing of Christ continues the wrath of God being poured out on the world. He treads the winepress of the fierceness and wrath of God (v. 15 above). It also shows that the armies of heaven come with Him, clothed in fine linen, white and clean (v. 14 above). Who are these? The use of the word 'white' may not completely distinguish the church, but I believe the word 'clean' does.

Revelation 17:14

"These will make war with the Lamb, and the Lamb will overcome them, for He is Lord of lords and King of kings; and those who are with Him are called, chosen, and faithful."

Those with the Son of Man at His appearing are His body, His bride, the church. These are the chosen by Him and called (Rom. 8:29-30, 9:22-24, Eph. 1:4-6, John 15:19, Rev. 17:14). Jude and Zechariah also tell us similar things:

Jude 1:14-15

"Now Enoch, the seventh from Adam, prophesied about these men also, saying, "Behold, the Lord comes with ten thousands of His saints, (15) to execute judgment on all, to convict all who

are ungodly among them of all their ungodly deeds which they have committed in an ungodly way, and of all the harsh things which ungodly sinners have spoken against Him."

Zechariah 14:5

"Then you shall flee through My mountain valley, For the mountain valley shall reach to Azal. Yes, you shall flee As you fled from the earthquake In the days of Uzziah king of Judah. Thus the Lord my God will come, And all the saints with You."

It is fairly clear that the church is with Christ when He appears, not on the earth experiencing the wrath of God along with the world. If we go to the passage quoted above from Revelation 19, we should notice what takes place previous to the Son of Man coming on the white horse. In Revelation 19:5-9 we have the marriage supper of the Lamb preceding His appearing to the world (Eph. 5:25-32). *"And to her it was granted to be arrayed in fine linen, clean and bright..."* The description of the church at the wedding feast matches that of the armies of heaven that follow Him on white horses (Rev. 19:14). It is obvious His bride, the church, is in heaven with Him in His Father's glory before He comes forth for judgment of the world.

General Biblical Principles help to properly explain Doctrine

The church world fails to understand general biblical principles that explain the counsels and plan of God. This leads to much error in teaching and doctrine. Here is an example of one biblical principle, if understood, bringing clarity to much of our teaching.

"...and the world has hated them because they are not of the world, just as I am not of the world."

This explains the position of the believer/church in contrast to all that is positioned with the world and of the world. The principle established is that Jesus is not of the world and is apart from the world. The believer/church is the same. We have no relationship with the world and are apart from it. The understanding of this principle and position establishes many spiritual truths we should be teaching. By this principle we are strangers and pilgrims on the earth, not connected here, and just passing through. By this principle we are constantly on a walk that eventually will take us out of this world. By this principle our walk is a following of Jesus out of this world, so that we may be where He is (John 12:25-26, 13:33-14:4). By this same principle, the Jews, as part of the world, simply cannot follow Him or end up where He is (John 7:33-34, 8:21).

John 8:23-24

"And He said to them, "You are from beneath; I am from above. You are of this world; I am not of this world. Therefore I said to you that you will die in your sins; for if you do not believe that I am He, you will die in your sins."

Here the Lord's words make the principle and difference in position quite clear. The believer/church is united to Christ and in His position. The exact same things said of Him can be said of us. *We are from above, Israel is from beneath. The Jews are of this world, but the believer/church is not of this world.* Therefore, by this established biblical principle as it relates to the church, it becomes inconceivable that we would teach the church will be on the earth during the tribulation when the wrath of God is being poured out on the world. This is not a proper understanding of the principle or the position. The true church is not of the world and its calling is above, not beneath. Israel is of this world and their calling is beneath. Israel cannot possibly go where the Lord had gone. But of the believer He says, "...you will follow Me afterward." (John 13:36)

After the Foundations of the World – part of the World

The proper understanding of this principle is vital because the principle itself is found over and over again in Scripture. All things revealed after the foundations of the world are simply part of the world by relationship. Therefore Israel is part of the world even though they were chosen and separated by God from the Gentiles. Their religion, given to the nation at Mt. Sinai to separate them from all the false religions of the Gentiles, is God's one religion of the earth – Judaism. The character of prophecy is God's dealings with the earth, His government of the earth, and promises and judgment of His earthly calling (Israel). The understandings of these ideas and this biblical principle are never compromised through all of Scripture.

The church, as apart from the world, will not be judged with the world. The body of Christ will not be on the earth during the coming tribulation – this would be the confounding of this biblical principle. Our calling is heavenly. It is not of the earth or of this world. Before God turns to judge the world, He will catch away the true church into the heavens.

The Biblical link between Judgment, Condemnation, and Wrath

In the Scriptures there is an obvious link between the three words – judgment, condemnation, and wrath. What we then find in Scriptures regarding these three words associated with the believer happens to be quite different in comparison to the position of the unbelieving world.

- As for judgment, God will judge the world (Rom. 2:2-5, 3:5-6, Rev. 14:7). All men will be judged according to their works (Rev. 20:12-15, Rom. 2:5-6). This is a guaranteed bad outcome. With the rejection of Christ the correct Biblical understanding is that God has already judged the world (John 12:31).

- As for condemnation – "...through one man's offence, judgment came to all men resulting in condemnation..." (Rom. 5:16, 18) "...but he who does not believe is condemned already, because he has not believed in the name of the only begotten Son of God." (John 3:18)

- As for wrath – *Romans 1:18 "For the wrath of God is revealed from heaven against all ungodliness and unrighteousness of men, who suppress the truth in unrighteousness,"* In physical birth, all men by nature are children of wrath (Eph. 2:3).

The Believer/Church's relationship to Judgment, Condemnation, and Wrath

If we look at the believer/church in view of these three biblical words we get a completely different story. As believers, what we should already understand and have settled in our hearts is that Jesus bore our sins (I Pet. 2:24). He was made to be sin for us (II Cor. 5:21). On the cross Jesus was judged by God and condemned (John 3:14). He experienced the pouring out of God's wrath on Himself, innocently. This was the cup that He struggled with in His own will to drink (Matt. 26:38-44). Christ did this all for us. So what we find when we search the Scriptures concerning these three words associated with the believer, it is quite different than the position of the unbelieving world.

- *For judgment: John 5:24 "Most assuredly, I say to you, he who hears My word and believes in Him who sent Me has everlasting life, and shall not come into judgment, but has passed from death into life."*

- *For condemnation: Romans 8:1 "There is therefore now no condemnation to those who are in Christ Jesus."*

- *For wrath: 1 Thessalonians 5:9 "For God did not appoint us to wrath, but to obtain salvation through our Lord Jesus Christ,"*

There is a practical effect that the blessed hope of the true believer/church has now in light of the three words above and the proper understanding of our biblical relationship to them. This practical effect is this – instead of looking at the future with fear and anxiety concerning God's condemnation and wrath, the whole character and expectation of Christ's return for us is changed. For the believer/church we will not experience God's judgment and fiery indignation, nor will the true church go through the coming tribulation as if we are Jacob in the midst of Jacob's trouble. The spirit and character of our waiting for Christ, His coming for us, and our gathering to Him, is one entirely removed from judgment, condemnation, and wrath. It is one of joy and peace, as well as excited anticipation and hope.

Jesus bore the judgment, condemnation, and wrath of God that was for us. He was delivered up because of our offences. He did this on the cross. He then was raised for our justification (Rom. 4:24-25). *"Therefore, having been justified by faith, we have peace with God through our Lord Jesus Christ...and rejoice in hope of the glory of God."* (Rom. 5:1-2) We have no need of judgment in order for Jesus to come and take us to our Father's house. There is no judgment that stands between the believer and his entrance into the glory of God.

The Mystery of Christ

The biblical principles established by God in His ways and counsels are vital understandings that are maintained in the unfolding of His plan. Jesus and the believer apart from the world is just one principle. Another important revealed truth is the mystery of Christ.

Romans 16:25

"Now to Him who is able to establish you according to my gospel and the preaching of Jesus Christ, according to the revelation of the mystery kept secret since the world began."

Ephesians 3:3-4

"...how that by revelation He made known to me the mystery (as I have briefly written already, by which, when you read, you may understand my knowledge in the mystery of Christ),"

Colossians 1:26-27

"...the mystery which has been hidden from ages and from generations, but now has been revealed to His saints. To them God willed to make known what are the riches of the glory of this mystery among the Gentiles: which is Christ in you, the hope of glory."

The mystery is given specifically to Paul by direct revelation from Christ. This would mean in face to face communication with Christ in glory (II Cor. 12:1-4). The gospel He preached came in the exact same way, by seeing and speaking to Christ in glory (Gal. 1:11-12).[37] That is the reason his gospel is called the gospel of the glory of Christ (II Cor. 4:4, I Tim. 1:11-12).

The mystery is Christ in you, the hope of glory. That is, for the believer individually, Christ lives in you and you live in Him, united by the Spirit. There is a living Christ in the believer (Gal. 2:20). He is our life (Col. 3:3-4). But the mystery is also that individual believers are united together by the Spirit into one body, and that this body is in union with the Head in glory, Jesus Christ (Eph. 1:19-23). The mystery is the fact of the existence of the body of Christ (Eph. 2:11-22). The mystery is all the doctrine concerning the existence of this mystical body. It includes all the teaching and instruction for His body, along with its proper calling and Christian hopes.

According to Romans 16:25 above, the revelation of the mystery was hidden from the time the world began. Its revelation was through Paul by the Spirit, after the Holy Spirit was sent (Eph. 3:2-5). This is when the revelation of the mystery was made known, and the instruments by which it was accomplished. To whom was it made known? – His saints (Col. 1:26). Yet it existed before the world in the counsels of God. It was simply kept hidden in God. If it preceded the world being created, then the mystery and all it contains has no relationship with the world. This shows the importance of understanding Biblical principles.

A Christ in Glory

The mystery of Christ was given only to Paul. It was not Peter's or John's responsibility. These two never teach one truth concerning the corporate body of Christ. The mystery was a personal dispensation or stewardship given to Paul alone (Eph. 3:8-11, Col. 1:24-27). It was his responsibility. For its building up on the earth by the hands of men, Paul alone, as a wise master builder, laid its solid foundation (I Cor. 3:10-11). Other ministers would build on this foundation that he placed for the building. All of these truths are dependent on a Christ in glory.

If you say the church is found in the Old Testament along with its teachings and doctrine, you would be arguing contrary to God and His Word. The Spirit says it was kept secret from the beginning of the world (Rom. 16:25). There are only non-descript types and shadows hinting at the church. Shadows are not real and do not produce doctrine. The revelation of the mystery was after Jesus Christ was exalted in glory and the Spirit sent down to reveal it.[38] Before that, it was hidden from the prophets and prophecy by God. If the mystery cannot be found in the Old Testament, then certainly its instructions and doctrine cannot be found there!

The Church World does not possess Sound Doctrine

If you apply to the church the teachings and instructions of Israel, you will quickly enter into error and unsound doctrine. You will be guilty of giving the church a different character and calling than that given by God. You will rob from the church its privilege and proper hopes. You will be Judaizing the Christian faith, joining it to the religion of the earth (Gal. 4:3, 9-11). You will do this by exalting man and diminishing the sovereign work of God, robbing glory from Him and giving man a reason to boast. You will not be turning the believer's attention to the midnight cry of His returning for the church to catch us away, but rather, it will all be about what man can build and accomplish on the earth. You will be guilty of helping the professing church say as Laodicea, "I am rich, have become wealthy, and have need of nothing." (Rev. 3:17) You will teach that the church endures the wrath of God in the tribulation right alongside the world. The denial of the mystery is a failure in spiritual understanding and doctrine, with only corrupt leaven as it fruit.

Revelation 14:10

"...he himself shall also drink of the wine of the wrath of God, which is poured out full strength into the cup of His indignation. He shall be tormented with fire and brimstone in the presence of the holy angels and in the presence of the Lamb."

The coming tribulation has the character of being the judgment of the world. God is the one who will judge and bring wrath. He is the holy and righteous God and He will judge the world according to His own nature and character.

Romans 1:18

"For the wrath of God is revealed from heaven against all ungodliness and unrighteousness of men, who suppress the truth in unrighteousness,"

Romans 2:5

"But in accordance with your hardness and your impenitent heart you are treasuring up for yourself wrath in the day of wrath and revelation of the righteous judgment of God,"

Romans 3:5-6

"But if our unrighteousness demonstrates the righteousness of God, what shall we say? Is God unjust who inflicts wrath? (I speak as a man.) Certainly not! For then how will God judge the world?"

The Believer/Church not appointed for Wrath

But the principle of the believer/church is that it is apart from the world. It is that Christ bore our sins, and the wrath of God that was due to us was upon Him.

John 3:36

He who believes in the Son has everlasting life; and he who does not believe the Son shall not see life, but the wrath of God abides on him."

Romans 5:9

Much more then, having now been justified by His blood, we shall be saved from wrath through Him.

The true believer/church is not appointed for wrath by God. This is a sound biblical thought, and also a promise from God in His word (I Thess. 5:9).

I Thess. 1:10

"...and to wait for His Son from heaven, whom He raised from the dead, even Jesus who delivers us from the wrath to come."

This 'wrath to come' could be seen as the coming tribulation, which will certainly be the wrath of God poured out on this evil and unbelieving world. Also coming is a final condemnation and wrath from God for the wicked after the white throne judgment. This is the lake of fire. Before this however, for the wicked and unbelieving, it is appointed for man once to die, after that the judgment – this is incarceration in Hades. At the white throne judgment Hades gives up its wicked dead to final judgment, which is the lake of fire (Rev. 20:11-15). However a thousand years before this, the coming tribulation on the earth is the wrath of God in executing judgment on the living world.

Israel and the Earth – both linked together and delivered by Judgment

There is a principle in Scripture and prophecy that Israel is connected to the earth. There is a legitimate thought that both the earth and Israel have a similarity in their separate salvations – both are delivered through judgment. The earth through the tribulation will endure the wrath of God. The earth is the battle zone between the devil who is kicked out of the heavens and down to the earth, apostate man wanting to rule and reign independently from God over the earth, and God who is the rightful God of the earth, having created it.

Israel, by the Jewish remnant, will be delivered through judgment and restored in the Promised Land. Everything about Israel is earthy – their religion, their calling, the seal of the remnant, their promises – all connect them to the earth. When the Jewish remnant is seen with the Lamb on Mt. Zion (Rev. 14:1-4) they are described as *the hundred and forty-four thousand who were redeemed from the earth.* In principle, both Israel with the earthly calling, and the earth itself, will be delivered through judgment (Jer. 30:7). The coming tribulation is mainly a Jewish judgment. It is spoken of as Jacob's trouble (Jer. 30:7). It is a time of trouble like none other seen on the face of the earth. It is on Daniel's people (Dan. 12:1), the Jews. The coming tribulation is God's dealings with the earth, and all that is connected and associated with it.

Ephesians 2:2-5

"...in which you once walked according to the course of this world, according to the prince of the power of the air, the spirit who now works in the sons of disobedience, (3) among whom also we all once conducted ourselves in the lusts of our flesh, fulfilling the desires of the flesh and of the mind, and were by nature children of wrath, just as the others."

(4) "But God, who is rich in mercy, because of His great love with which He loved us, (5) even when we were dead in trespasses, made us alive together with Christ (by grace you have been saved),"

In Adam, by natural birth, we are all children of wrath. We are all sons of disobedience. We can see in the Scriptures that it is on the sons of disobedience that the wrath of God will be poured out. But it is obvious from the above passage that the position of the believer/ church is no longer being sons of disobedience. We are no longer children of wrath. We are delivered 'from' the wrath to come, not 'out of' the wrath to come. We are now the children of God, the sons of obedience.

Ephesians 5:6

Let no one deceive you with empty words, for because of these things the wrath of God comes upon the sons of disobedience.

Colossians 3:6

Because of these things the wrath of God is coming upon the sons of disobedience,

Sons of disobedience or sons of God? What is the position of the believer and true church?

Matthew 24:29-30

"Immediately after the tribulation of those days the sun will be darkened, and the moon will not give its light; the stars will fall from heaven, and the powers of the heavens will be shaken. Then the sign of the Son of Man will appear in heaven, and then all the tribes of the earth will mourn, and they will see the Son of Man coming on the clouds of heaven with power and great glory."

There is no doubt that the appearing or manifestation of Christ to the world brings an end to the tribulation period. Also there should be no doubt that the church comes with Him in His glory at this time, and that the church appears or is manifested with Him to the world. Further, in the next chapter, we will understand how His appearing brings an end to this present age, and the Son of Man sitting on His throne of glory in Jerusalem is the start of the next.

Chapter 12: Endnotes

[36] Mathew's gospel is the Messianic and Jewish gospel. It is different in its character and flavor than the other two synoptic gospels. In Matthew, Christ is presented from the outset as the accomplishment of promises and prophecies to the nation of Israel. Therefore you see the frequent use of the phrase, 'that it might be fulfilled what was written by the prophets'. (Matt. 1:22) However, unique to Matthew's gospel is all the teaching concerning 'the kingdom of heaven' that was at hand. This makes his gospel, in a sense, the dispensational gospel. If we hold the idea of a Jewish dispensation, then it is shown in Matthew as suspended and set aside, while something different was about to be brought forth – the kingdom of heaven and the part of God's counsels dealing with heavenly things. The kingdom of heaven is always at hand in Matthew, for it does not exist until the Son of Man was raised and glorified, and went away back to heaven. The existence of the kingdom of heaven and all its teachings (Matt. 13:51-52) are solely related to the title of the Son of Man. None of its teachings or its understandings are related to the title of Messiah, Messianic prophecies, or prophecy in general.

Messiah is a title from out of prophecy, and is strictly for Israel. It has many prophetic promises attached to the title, according to the prophetic writings and law, which are inseparable from it: throne of David, twelve tribes of Israel restored in the Promised Land stretching in expanse from the Nile to the Euphrates rivers, and all Gentile rule cast off. Israel, as restored, will prosper and multiply in the land under their Messiah and Prince, and they will become the greatest nation on the face of the earth during the millennium. All these promises and more are for Israel, on the earth, and according to 'known' prophecy. Also the Jews, their leaders, and the Lord's own disciples, properly and correctly understood that when Messiah came to Israel, He would remain forever – again according to the writings in the law and prophets (John 12:34).

Some people say that His suffering, crucifixion, and death were clearly associated with the Messiah title, and done so in Jewish prophecy. If this is true it sets up some peculiar thoughts in my mind. Not only am I thinking that every human being on the face of the earth at that time totally misunderstood the purpose of the coming of Messiah to Israel, including His own disciples, but also another strange thought – if Israel's leaders and people would have properly understood prophecy, then they all should have been looking for their Messiah for the purpose of putting Him to death and therefore fulfilling the prophecies. This conclusion is borderline absurdity. Yet this is the logical reasoning of anyone's mind who believes that His death is connected with the Messiah title of prophecy.

Jesus always associates His death, resurrection, and exaltation to the right hand of God with His title as the Son of Man. This title is the second Adam, the last Man, and by Psalm 8 is related and connected to the first Adam. The Son of Man is the antitype of the first Adam, and is the heavenly Man in comparison to the earthly man (I Cor. 15:47). However, Messiah is the son of David according to prophecy and coming in the flesh; very Jewish in character and blessings. If His death was connected to the title of Messiah as some say, then Israel did right by putting their Messiah to death. Again an absurd thought, but the logical conclusion to the aforementioned belief.

What wasn't found as revealed in known prophecy? What was hidden from the prophets? What was new revelation in Matthew's gospel? Instead of the kingdom of God in Israel with Emmanuel physically present as their Messiah (what was known), it is 'the kingdom of heaven is at hand' and the Son of Man going away (what was not known). Also hidden from prophecy and the prophets is the spoiled crop of wheat and tares in the field of the world (Matt. 13:24-30). Why are these things hidden from prophecy? There are a number of Biblical reasons why, but one that is easiest to see is that all three have a direct connection to the church (the body of Christ), which is definitely hidden from prophecy (Eph. 3:1-6). The church does not exist until the Son of Man went away and was glorified (Eph. 1:18-23). The spoiled crop in the world includes the body of Christ – the wheat. And all the heavenly parts of the term 'kingdom of heaven' involve only the true church. In Matthew then, the transition from the prophetic title of Messiah to that of the Son of Man is seen in the differences between the kingdom of God present in Israel and the coming kingdom of heaven.

The Jewish character of Matthew's gospel is readily seen in the entire twenty-fourth chapter containing the Lord's prophetic statements – the subject is Judea, Jerusalem, and the temple. This parallels Daniel's 70 week prophecy found in Daniel 9:24-27, which also is about Judea, Jerusalem, the temple, and the Jews found there. Both of these prophecies are very similar to each other, localized in their scope, and barely hint at Gentile involvement. Both passages are truly about Jacob's trouble – the last three and a half years of the tribulation.

When compared to John's gospel the differences are even more striking and profound. John's gospel is more the believer's gospel because the world and Israel are set aside in the very first chapter (John 1:5, 10-11). Israel is spoken to by Christ as part of the world and set aside through the entire gospel. Then there are His long discourses spoken to His disciples when they are away from the people (John 13-17). The disciples represent all believers. There are other characteristics of John's gospel: the manifestation in the flesh of the Son sent down from heaven, who reveals the Father. This is also decidedly Christian truth and revelation, and not Jewish.

[37] Paul's apostleship was not from any man or group of men (i.e. the other apostles). He conclusively establishes this in the first verse of the book of Galatians, effectively telling us the viewpoint from which he writes this specific epistle that combats the Judaizing leaven that corrupts Christianity.

Galatians 1:1

"Paul, an apostle (not from men nor through man, but through Jesus Christ and God the Father who raised Him from the dead),"

The false teaching of apostolic succession and its accompanying heresies of infallibility and church authority are debunked in this one verse of the apostle's pithy greeting to the Galatians.

[38] The church doesn't exist until Jesus Christ was exalted to the right hand of God (Eph. 1:20-23). When this occurred the Holy Spirit was sent down to gather the body. Believers were not given the Holy Spirit until after Jesus was glorified (John 7:39). The Spirit dwelling in the believer is what makes him a son of God (Eph. 1:13, Gal. 3:26, 4:6-7, Rom. 8:14-17). By this same Spirit the corporate body was formed (I Cor. 12:12-13) – by one Spirit we were all baptized into one body.

Notes

Chapter 13:

This Present Evil Age

A day or so before the crucifixion Jesus left the temple after teaching and sat with His disciples on the Mount of Olives. The temple and associated buildings were within eyesight and some of the disciples pointed their beauty out to the Lord. This is when Jesus made a dramatic prophetic statement referring to the coming destruction of the temple and Jerusalem.

Matthew 24:2

"And Jesus said to them, "Do you not see all these things? Assuredly, I say to you, not one stone shall be left here upon another, that shall not be thrown down.""

This was fulfilled in 70 AD when the Roman armies leveled Jerusalem to the ground. Jesus speaks in greater detail about this event and the period of time leading up to it. It would serve as a prophetic warning to the early church, particularly the church in Jerusalem. It was a warning that would keep every hair of their heads from being lost (Luke 21:18). This detail of instruction is found in two passages of Scripture: one in Mark and one in Luke.

Mark 13:9-13

"But watch out for yourselves, for they will deliver you up to councils, and you will be beaten in the synagogues. You will be brought before rulers and kings for My sake, for a testimony to them. (10) And the gospel must first be preached to all the nations. (11) But when they arrest you and deliver you up, do not worry beforehand, or premeditate what you will speak. But whatever is given you in that hour, speak that; for it is not you who speak, but the Holy Spirit. (12) Now brother will betray brother to death, and a father his child; and children will rise up against parents and cause them to be put to death. (13) And you will be hated by all for My name's sake. But he who endures to the end shall be saved."

The Time-jumping characteristic to some Prophetic Passages

This passage is framed by other portions of prophecy that specifically point to a different time altogether. It is a sort of time-jumping that is characteristic of many prophetic passages. An example of this can easily be seen in a different prophecy in Isaiah concerning the Messianic Kingdom (Is. 9:6-7).[39] The Lord's preceding words in Mark 13:5-8 are about the beginning of the coming tribulation and are directed to the future remnant, not His current disciples. The portion that starts in Mark 13:14 again jumps forward to the tribulation period – the sign that begins the last three and a half years of that period.[40] It is a portion which is also specifically directed as instruction to the future Jewish remnant. But verses 9-13 are definitely spoken to His present disciples, warning them of coming persecution and hardship in their ministry, and the general scope of events leading up to the destruction of the city by the Romans in 70 AD. The gospel at that time was taken to the nations by Paul, who is definitely in the Lord's thoughts when He mentions a testimony before rulers and kings.

Luke 21:12-24

"But before all these things, they will lay their hands on you and persecute you, delivering you up to the synagogues and prisons. You will be brought before kings and rulers for My name's sake. (13) But it will turn out for you as an occasion for testimony. (14) Therefore settle it in your hearts not to meditate beforehand on what you will answer; (15) for I will give you a mouth and wisdom which all your adversaries will not be able to contradict or resist. (16) You will be betrayed even by parents and brothers, relatives and friends; and they will put some of you to death. (17) And you will be hated by all for My name's sake. (18) But not a hair of your head shall be lost. (19) By your patience possess your souls."

(20) "But when you see Jerusalem surrounded by armies, then know that its desolation is near. (21) Then let those who are in Judea flee to the mountains, let those who are in the midst of her depart, and let not those who are in the country enter her. (22) For these are the days of vengeance, that all things which are written may be fulfilled. (23) But woe to those who are pregnant and to those who are nursing babies in those days! For there will be great distress in the land and wrath upon this people. (24) And they will fall by the edge of the sword, and be led away captive into all nations. And Jerusalem will be trampled by Gentiles until the times of the Gentiles are fulfilled."

As we found in Mark, this passage from Luke is framed with the same elements of time-jumping common to prophetic language. His preceding words in Luke 21:8-11 point to the beginning of the coming tribulation, while verses 25-36 point to His return that ends the tribulation of those days. However, the passage above is for His disciples and the early church in Jerusalem. The armies surrounding Jerusalem in verse 20 identify the event as the destruction of Jerusalem and the temple in 70 AD. His words leading up to this verse (vs. 12-19) are the same general warnings to His present disciples that we read in Mark. What He adds in verses 20-24 speaks of the destruction itself and God setting aside, for a time, the calling of Israel as a people of God. By these last few verses (vs. 20-24) we are assured we are talking about the 70 AD event. This was when the remaining Jews were 'led away captive into all nations.'

The Major Prophetic Passages from the Synoptic Gospels

i.   Jesus' first words reference the coming tribulation period and are spoken directly to the end-time Jewish remnant. They will serve as words of warning to His elect. These passages are Luke 21:8-11 and Mark 13:5-8.

ii.   In these same passages Jesus then switches back in time to talk prophetically to His present disciples, warning them concerning the time period leading up to the destruction of the city and temple by the Roman armies in 70 AD (Luke 21:6 and Mark 13:2). These passages are Luke 21:12-24 and Mark 13:9-13.

iii. In these same passages Jesus now jumps forward again to the time of the signs of His return to this world (Luke) or the sign that marks the last three and a half years leading up to His physical return (Mark). These passages again contain words that will serve as direct warnings to the future Jewish remnant. These passages are Luke 21:25-36 and Mark 13:14-37

iv.   Matthew's gospel is the gospel of Messiah and is very Jewish in its character.[41] The prophetic passage in Matt. 24:4-44 all concerns the time of Jacob's trouble or the time immediately preceding it in the end. There isn't anything in that passage that *specifically* refers to His current disciples.

How would we define this Present Evil Age?

What I want to look more closely at is what is referred to in Scripture as this present age. When Jesus sat down on the Mount of Olives His disciples came and asked three questions (Matt. 24:3). The first was, "Tell us when will these things be?" This we have already discussed, for it refers to the destruction of Jerusalem that was to come shortly. The second and third questions are asked together. "And what will be the sign of Your coming, and the end of the age?" The appearing of the Son of Man to the world is what in fact ends this present age. But how might we define the age, its parameters and character?

1.) We would be tempted to call it the Christian age, or the age of the gospel, but this wouldn't be correct. All Christ's answers concern the subjects of prophecy. It is all about the temple, Jerusalem, and Israel. It is about Jacob's trouble, references to Daniel, and His second coming as Messiah and the Son of Man. His words are so much more Jewish than Christian.

2.) We might then be tempted to call this the Jewish age. We could point to Daniel's 70 week prophecy which is decidedly about Jerusalem, the temple, and the Jewish people (Dan. 9:24). However it's not likely a prophecy would start an age without some historic event. The 70 week prophecy basically begins in the middle of Cyrus' reign with the rebuilding of Jerusalem after Nebuchadnezzar had destroyed it. Also, this prophecy has a suspension or parenthesis between the 69th and 70th week that isn't easily explained by the thought of a Jewish age.

3.) It is the first prophecy in the book of Daniel, Nebuchadnezzar's dream (Dan. 2:27-36), that defines and describes the present age. This dream is from man's viewpoint – a great image whose splendor was excellent, whose form was awesome (v. 31).

This Present Age – the Times of the Gentiles

How can I be so sure this is the present age? I believe in the passage quoted above Jesus defines the age as 'the times of the Gentiles.' (Luke 21:24) And we should not mistakenly define the age from the time Rome sacked Jerusalem all the way to Christ's return. Rather it is from the time Nebuchadnezzar destroyed Jerusalem and took Judah captive. This is when the world dominion of Gentile power begins. God sets up the Gentiles to rule the known world throughout the entire age. The statue of the king's dream defines the age of the Gentile world dynasties – a.k.a. 'the times of the Gentiles.'

What other evidence of this present age brings us to make these same conclusions? Jerusalem will be trampled by Gentiles until the times of the Gentiles are fulfilled. When will we know these times are fulfilled? He tells us in the next few verses.

Luke 21:25-27

"And there will be signs in the sun, in the moon, and in the stars; and on the earth distress of nations, with perplexity, the sea and the waves roaring; (26) men's hearts failing them from fear and the expectation of those things which are coming on the earth, for the powers of the heavens will be shaken. (27) Then they will see the Son of Man coming in a cloud with power and great glory."

The destruction of the Gentile Statue

The 'times of the Gentiles' come to an end in the same way that the coming tribulation ends – with the advent of the Son of Man from heaven. This is the end of the tribulation and this is the end of the age. This truth is confirmed in Daniel's vision of the four Gentile beasts – *"One like the Son of Man, coming with the clouds of heaven."* (Dan. 7:13) It is also confirmed in the ending of the king's dream.

Daniel 2:34-35

"You watched while a stone was cut out without hands, which struck the image on its feet of iron and clay, and broke them in pieces. (35) Then the iron, the clay, the bronze, the silver, and the gold were crushed together, and became like chaff from the summer threshing floors; the wind carried them away so that no trace of them was found. And the stone that struck the image became a great mountain and filled the whole earth."

The stone cut out without hands is the Son of Man from heaven. Christ returns and strikes the Gentile statue in its feet – the final form of the fourth beast as depicted in Rev. 13:1-7. The feet of iron and clay are the form the fourth beast assumes at the end of the Gentile age, ascending out of the bottomless pit (Rev. 17:8, 11:7). The feet are completely destroyed by the stone. The scene of this destruction is depicted in graphic detail in Rev. 19:15-21 – it is 'the supper of the great God.' In the king's dream there is no trace left of any remaining Gentile rule, power, or dominion, as the entire statue is ground up into chaff by the Son of Man.

An Age of Gentile Civil Power

What else might we say is characteristic of the age? This period of time starts after the presence and glory of Jehovah leaves Jerusalem and its temple and the earth (Ez. 10:18-19). When the age ends, the presence and glory of Jehovah will return to Jerusalem and to a new millennial temple (Ez. 43:1-6). This is a biblical principle of great importance to recognize relating to the glory of Jehovah physically present on earth in Israel and government of the world. This present age itself is one of Gentile civil power, the principle of God's government taken away from Israel and given to the Gentiles. *It is a period of time between when the presence and glory of God was in Israel, and when it will be again in the future.* It is a time of testing of responsibility for the Gentiles. However, being man in Adam, their testing had predictable results. The Gentiles use civil power to exalt themselves and work unrighteousness, not to honor God and do His will. The characteristic behavior of Gentile civil world power is depicted by God as beasts and can easily be understood from a few passages from Daniel.

Daniel 4:30

"The king spoke, saying, "Is not this great Babylon, that I have built for a royal dwelling by my mighty power and for the honor of my majesty?"

The beast character is one of iniquity, pride, and self-exaltation. But particularly it is independence from the will of God or in any way answering to God. It simply does its own thing, goes its own way, and does its own will. The beasts do not acknowledge the Most High God. Immediately after the above passage was spoken by Nebuchadnezzar God judges him, making him behave as a beast for seven years.

This character of a beast disappears when he is made to acknowledge God (Dan. 4:31-37). This in itself is an important principle to understand – how the character of the beast is made to disappear. The example of Nebuchadnezzar's judgment ending shows this prophetic principle. It is this principle that is the only means of properly explaining the three distinct epochs of the fourth beast – the Roman Empire (Rev. 17:8).

Daniel 8:4

"I saw the ram pushing westward, northward, and southward, so that no animal could withstand him; nor was there any that could deliver from his hand, but he did according to his will and became great.

The ram is a symbolic beast depicting the Medo-Persian Empire that succeeded Babylon. We easily see the characteristic beast behavior. It does its own will independent from God.

Gentile failure in responsibility in Civil Power

In civil power and dominion the Gentiles bring in other characteristics. Three prominent failures can be seen in the first three kings of the age.

1. The first king, Nebuchadnezzar, institutes kingdom wide idolatry (Dan. 3:1-7).[42]

2. The second king, Belshazzar, blasphemes God by his use of the temple vessels that are holy and sanctified to Him, even in captivity (Dan. 5:1-5).

3. The third king, Darius the Mede, makes himself a god to be worshiped (Dan. 6:6-9).

The Gentile idolatry, blasphemy, and self-deification are evils that run through the entire age. All the Caesars of the time of the fourth beast were prone to all three, just in a worsening display. If you closely examine the final form of the fourth beast that ascends out of the bottomless pit in the tribulation period, along with the second beast from the earth, you will see the full ripening of these evils for the end of the age (Rev. 13). In principle this is what evil does – it never improves, it only worsens, and in the end its full ripening is its perfection.

The end of the Gentile age will result in the greatest displays of evil this world has ever seen (Matt. 24:21). And this is for good reason – the dragon, with its seven heads, the perfection of evil, is cast down to the earth and comes with great wrath, for he knows his time is short (Rev. 12:7-13). The two beasts of Revelation 13 are then given the dragon's full authority and power, and the first beast his earthly throne. All this is another characteristic of the present age.

Satan established in the Heavens

When God was present in Israel, God ruled the earth by direct government. His throne was the ark behind the veil in the tabernacle or Solomon's temple. Leaving the earth, He turned direct government over to the Gentiles. God is seen in Daniel as He who overrules all things providentially. In Daniel He is called the God of heaven (Dan. 4:25-26), but not the God of the world and the earth. When the presence and glory of Jehovah left Israel and the earth, Satan became the god of this world, of this earth, and of this present age. He could not have had these titles while the glory of Jehovah was still present in Israel. But with the onset of Gentile civil world power Satan is established in the heavens (not 'the' heaven were the throne of God resides – Rev. 4:2).[43]

Ephesians 6:12

"For we do not wrestle against flesh and blood, but against principalities, against powers, against the rulers of the darkness of this age, against spiritual hosts of wickedness in the heavenly places."

The principalities and powers are angelic administrations. They are rulers of the evil of this present age. There are angels of wickedness in the heavens. If Satan is later cast down to the earth (Rev. 12:7-12), then his authority, power, and influence is presently established in the heavens. We first see these spiritual realities of the age in the book of Daniel (Dan. 10:10-21), with Gabriel struggling against the prince of the kingdoms of Persia and Greece.

Eph. 2:2

"...in which you once walked according to the course of this world, according to the prince of the power of the air, the spirit who now works in the sons of disobedience."

Satan, the god of this Gentile Age

Although the phrase 'the course of this world' brings a certain beneficial understanding to the beginning part of this verse, a better translation may be 'the age of this world.' Paul is speaking of this present age and Satan as the god controlling it. The age has a certain progress and course of ripening evil that is under his influence. The prince of the power of the air is Satan established as spiritual wickedness in the heavens.

2 Corinthians 4:4

"...whose minds the god of this age has blinded, who do not believe, lest the light of the gospel of the glory of Christ, who is the image of God, should shine on them."

Ephesians 1:21

"...far above all principality and power and might and dominion, and every name that is named, not only in this age but also in that which is to come."

Satan definitely came to be the god of this present age. The principalities and powers are the spiritual wickedness established in the heavens influencing the development and character of the age. The Scriptures show that this age progresses in evil to its end. However the believer, being in Christ, is no longer part of this age, as he is not part of this world.

Galatians 1:3-5

"Grace to you and peace from God the Father and our Lord Jesus Christ, who gave Himself for our sins, that He might deliver us from this present evil age, according to the will of our God and Father, to whom be glory forever and ever. Amen.

The return of the Son of Man in power and glory will mean the end of all Gentile rule and dominion. Satan and his wicked spirits will be bound from the earth. The living in the world will be judged. The curse and corruption of creation will be lifted. The age that follows will be the Son of Man sitting on His throne of glory reigning in righteousness and peace. This is how this present age will end and a glimpse of the character and differences of the age to come.

Delivered from this Present Evil Age

But Christ has given Himself for us that He might deliver us from this present evil age. The believer has been delivered and set apart from it, although we still walk on this earth in the midst of it. We should know what the evil age looks like because we should be taught and grounded in the Scriptures. When the believer identifies evil and corruption, he is always instructed in the Word of God to turn from it (II Tim. 2:19, 22, 3:5).

The Progress of Evil

We cannot stop the progression of this present evil age. God Himself does not stretch forth His right arm of power to stop it. He tells us about its progression in the Scriptures. We see it in Daniel. We can read about its final form in Revelations. We should be listening to Paul's warnings in the epistles (Acts 20:17-31, II Tim. 3:1-5, 13, 4:3-4). Do these passages mean the believer/church ought to be able to stop it? When Jesus entered the world it did not know Him and eventually rejected Him. He did not change it or save it, but condemned the world at that time (John 12:31). The Scriptures simply mean what they say and reveal, and contain the mind and ways of God concerning these things. We ought to take the Scriptures more seriously. They teach that the evil ripens until the end. It is the character of this present evil age. The believer/church cannot stop it. Your prayers will not stop it. Your prayers would not be in line with the Word of God.

The Mind of God

We think we can change the world. We think we can save the world. We think we can change and save America. It is all exaggerated thoughts and prayers. It is man trying to feel like he does something important by which he will exalt himself. God has already condemned the world that you say you can change and save. How is this the mind of God? How does this line up with revealed Scripture? The age is following its evil course. The world follows the course of this age. The believer/church cannot steer it otherwise.

There are certain things we can be doing as believers. We share and preach the gospel as God directs, and see who God is drawing to Christ (John 6:44). By this God uses us as instruments of His grace in what He is doing. The one thing that remains as far as the true wheat and the Lord returning for us is the term Paul uses (Rom. 11:25) – until the 'fullness of the Gentiles comes in'. This fullness is a quantity entering the body of Christ that only the Father would know. This is one of the reasons why the early church constantly expected the Lord's return for them in their days. It is why the Thessalonians mistakenly feared that those believers among them who had fallen asleep (died) had lost any hope of being included in the rapture event (I Thess. 4:13). Paul assures them this is not true, that when Christ comes for the church, God will bring with Him those who sleep in Jesus (I Thess. 4:14). The rapture event means the resurrection of those who have fallen asleep in Christ. Those of us that remain alive will by no means precede those who are asleep (I Thess. 4:15).

By the redemptive work of the Son of Man, we have been delivered from this present evil age, and this, according to the will of God our Father (Gal. 1:4). Before the ending fireworks of the coming tribulation, before the end of this present age, our Father will send the Son to catch up His body and bring it glorified into His presence. Will this not be deliverance from this present evil age? It is the blessed hope of the church. It is the believer's constant expectation.

Chapter 13: Endnotes

[39] In Isaiah 9:6-7 you have 'unto us a Child is born' – this is spoken by Israel, but more importantly and in a greater spiritual reality, it belongs to the future Jewish remnant. This remnant is what Jesus saves in the end, as far as the nation of Israel is involved in the counsels of God. They are the ones who truly say, 'unto us a Son is given.' These are the ones in Israel who will see the government upon His shoulders.

But certainly a Child born refers to an event 2000 years ago, at least in some measure. If we discuss the government upon the Son's shoulders, then we are jumping forward in time. This is characteristic of many prophetic passages. Another example of this is in the great image in the dream of Nebuchadnezzar found in Dan. 2:31-36. In v. 33 it says, "Its legs of iron, its feet partly of iron and partly of clay." The legs of iron represent the Roman Empire in the time of the first appearance of Messiah to Israel. The feet are yet future, when the Roman Empire will be revived and in power again, and when Messiah will be presented to Israel a second time.

There are many examples we can find in prophecy that have this feature – 'time jumping' – and there is an obvious reason for it. All of the time-jumping in prophetic passages are jumping over the same thing. They are all by-passing the mystery of Christ (Eph. 3:3-5, 9), and the time of God's dealing with heavenly things. The mystery was kept secret since the world began (Rom. 16:25). Therefore, the mystery has no connection with the world and is not of the world. This is one reason it cannot be found in prophecy, because prophecy is about the world and the earth, and the earthly calling. The mystery simply doesn't fit in prophecy, and would violate biblical principles if we force it there. That is why prophecy always skips over the time of the mystery.

Actually, when Israel was set aside by God with the rejection of Jesus Christ as their Messiah, both prophecy and time ground to a halt. Prophecy is about Israel and God's government of the earth. Time in Scripture only relates to Israel in the counsels of God. Therefore, we see that presently, time is not being counted, the earth is not being dealt with, and prophecy is not being fulfilled. *As long as God is still dealing with His mystery, all these elements are suspended.* As long as the true wheat remain in the spoiled crop in the field (the world), having not yet been gathered up and removed from the field (the rapture), and placed into His barn (heaven), then these things remain on the sidelines (Matt. 13:30). These understandings are sound biblical principles found in God's Word as taught by the Spirit.

[40] The 'abomination of desolation' spoken of by Daniel marks the middle of the final seven years (one week) of counted time towards unbelieving Israel. The antichrist will confirm a covenant with the nation for one week (7 years – John 5:43), but will make an abomination in the middle of the week, bringing an end to sacrifices and offerings in the temple (Dan. 9:27).

[41] Matthew's gospel is the Messianic gospel. In it, Christ is presented from the outset as the accomplishment of Old Testament prophetic statements and promises. It is the character of this gospel. The phrasing, 'that it might be fulfilled which was spoken by the Lord through the prophet, saying...' is used constantly (Matt. 1:22, 2:5, 2:15, 17, 3:3...). Matthew presents Jesus Christ as Immanuel the Messiah, the Lord in the midst of Israel. And this is always very earthly and physical in its nature (Matt. 11:2-5). The gospel that Jesus and His disciples preached was that of the kingdom of God now present by the presence of Immanuel in Israel, a kingdom heralded by its forerunner, John the Baptist, preparing the way of Jehovah (Luke 3:2-6, Matt. 3:3). The presentation of Messiah to Israel is found in Luke 4:17-29 and the gospel of Messiah they preached was the kingdom of God present among them (Luke 4:43, 8:1, and 9:1-6, 9:60 - 10:11). This preaching of the kingdom of God was restricted to Israel (Matt. 10:5-6, 11:1, 15:24-26) and included Messiah providing the children's bread to the nation – physical healing, physical deliverance, and feeding of the poor.

Having said all this about Messiah we must realize that 'Messiah' is a title taken up by the Son of God to fulfill a work in the counsels of God. But Messiah was rejected by Israel. They would not have Him as King. As such there would be no kingdom of God through the Messiah in Israel at that time. At His rejection, Israel's house would remain desolate for a long time (Matt. 23:37-39). This is the setting aside of the title of Messiah along with all the promises associated with it in the counsels of God. Along with this, Israel is set aside in the principle of the calling of God, their city and temple would be destroyed, and the practice of Judaism stopped. Prophecy stops. God ceases His dealings with the earth, the earthly calling in Israel, and earthly things of the kingdom of God (John 3:12).

If Messiah is set aside, there would be need for the counsels of God to turn to something different. This would be the title of the Son of Man and His suffering and death. The redemptive work is what is associated with the Son of Man title, along with His resurrection and glorification to the right hand of God. The gospel associated with this title is one of crucifixion and death (I Cor. 2:2, 15:1-4). What follows His death is all that God does to glorify the Son of Man (John 13:31-32), having been glorified by His death.

This transition from Messiah to the Son of Man, from the earthly physical blessings and mission of Messiah to that of the redemptive death of the other, is uniquely shown in Matthew's gospel. Instead of the kingdom of God through a Messiah in the flesh to Israel, God's counsels transition to the kingdom of heaven dependent on the Son of Man crucified, resurrected, and gone away to heaven (Matt. 13:24, 37, 25:14, Luke 19:11-12). The use of the phrase 'the kingdom of heaven' is exclusive to Matthew's gospel. John the Baptist, Jesus, and the disciples all declare that 'the kingdom of heaven is a hand,' because it doesn't exist until the Son of Man is resurrected and gone away into glory. The kingdom of heaven as described by the Lord in word and parables cannot be found anywhere in prophecy. The kingdom of heaven contains a mystery of God's that is hidden from prophecy and the prophets. This is the transition in the counsels of God as it is described in this way so uniquely in Matthew's gospel.

In summary: In Matthew's gospel John the Baptist, Jesus, and His disciples emphatically put forth a unique and different declaration, "the kingdom of heaven is at hand" (Matt. 3:2, 4:17, 10:7, and 13:24-30). This is a new revelation involving an entirely different kind of kingdom, and all centered on the title and role of Jesus as the Son of Man raised and glorified (Matt. 13:37). This is of importance for properly understanding the revelation and character of this kingdom and God's counsels concerning it.

[42] Israel was filled with idolatry in the time of Elijah. The kingdom of Israel was scattered by the Assyrian into the nations. The kingdom of Judah fared slightly better and remained in the land longer. Eventually they were taken captive to Babylon. This is when the nation of Israel was delivered from its unclean spirit of idolatry (Matt. 12:43-45). They haven't practiced idolatry for a long time now. But the spirit that went out of Israel is just biding its time and going through dry places. The unclean spirit of idolatry will return to the nation of Israel at the end of the age during the tribulation. Only then it will be seven more spirits more wicked than the first (Matt. 12:45). This will be the last state of unbelieving Israel.

[43] Another viewpoint is that Satan became the god of this world after the crucifixion of Christ. The God who created the world had entered the world only to be rejected by the world (John 1:10). In the cross the

world thinks it had victory. The cross represents the hatred of the world against God fully manifested, and it represents the full power of Satan and darkness against Christ. But it was not Satan's victory as the world believes. To God and the eye of faith it is the resounding defeat of Satan, who held the power of death (Heb. 2:14-15). At the cross the Prince of this world was cast out, and the world was condemned (John 12:31-32). For believers, we patiently wait for the complete physical reality of this declared and set judgment to come to pass, both for the world and Satan. This physical reality is the subject of the book of Revelation.

However, Satan seems to have established authority previous to the cross. When he met Jesus in the temptation in the wilderness, he offers Him the kingdoms of the world as his to give as he pleases (Matt. 4:8-10). This certainly was a real temptation for he possessed these to give in exchange for worshipping him. The three temptations by Satan (Matt. 4:1-11) are all of the Son of God as the Son of Man. They have no inference to the Messiah title.

Notes

Chapter 14:

Christ, the Power and Wisdom of God

1 Corinthians 1:17-24

"For Christ did not send me to baptize, but to preach the gospel, not with wisdom of words, lest the cross of Christ should be made of no effect. (18) For the message of the cross is foolishness to those who are perishing, but to us who are being saved it is the power of God. (19) For it is written:

"I will destroy the wisdom of the wise,
And bring to nothing the understanding of the prudent."

(20) Where is the wise? Where is the scribe? Where is the disputer of this age? Has not God made foolish the wisdom of this world? (21) For since, in the wisdom of God, the world through wisdom did not know God, it pleased God through the foolishness of the message preached to save those who believe. (22) For Jews request a sign, and Greeks seek after wisdom; (23) but we preach Christ crucified, to the Jews a stumbling block and to the Greeks foolishness, (24) but to those who are called, both Jews and Greeks, Christ the power of God and the wisdom of God."

his was the state and condition of the world in the time when Paul preached his gospel (Rom. 16:25). In a general way it divides the unbelieving world into two distinct entities: unbelieving Jews and unbelieving Gentiles. It also defines a certain human mindset, distinct to each group, which is the main cause of their rejection of Christ. It is the general character of the world at that time. This character does not change for the good, but only worsens to the end.

Judaism – the Religion of the Flesh

The Jews are engulfed in their religion of the flesh. It only produces the confidences of the flesh (Phil. 3:2-6). It is a walk in the flesh, by senses, by sight, and by seeking signs. "For the Jews request a sign..." Their circumcision in the flesh is a sign and symbol to themselves that they are separate from the Gentiles. A Messiah to Israel crucified by their own hands on a cross is simply a stumbling stone, a reason of offence to this people (Rom. 9:30-33, Is. 8:14-15). This does not line up with their Messianic prophecies or what they expected and were looking for (John 12:34, Luke 18:31-34, Is. 9:6-7). Even today it still doesn't line up with what they are looking for.

Before the future appearing of Jesus Christ to the world, what will the condition of the nation of Israel be like? One very clear understanding from Scripture describes their condition as a nation from the time of Messiah's first appearing to them until He appears again.

Luke 13:34-35

"O Jerusalem, Jerusalem, the one who kills the prophets and stones those who are sent to her! How often I wanted to gather your children together, as a hen gathers her brood under her wings, but you were not willing! See! Your house is left to you desolate; and assuredly, I say to you, you shall not see Me until the time comes when you say, 'Blessed is He who comes in the name of the Lord!'"

Israel set aside until the end

Israel is a desolate nation. As a people they are set aside by God. He does not presently acknowledge their calling as a people of God. He says to them, "You are not my people, and I am not your God." (Hosea 1:9) The clear understanding from Jesus, their Messiah, is that they remain in this condition until He returns again to them[44] – the appearing of Christ to the world is His appearing to rescue a Jewish remnant from out of unbelieving Israel.

Matthew 24:15-26

"Therefore when you see the 'abomination of desolation,' spoken of by Daniel the prophet, standing in the holy place" (whoever reads, let him understand), (16) "then let those who are in Judea flee to the mountains. (17) Let him who is on the housetop not go down to take anything out of his house. (18) And let him who is in the field not go back to get his clothes. (19) But woe to those who are pregnant and to those who are nursing babies in those days! (20) And pray that your flight may not be in winter or on the Sabbath. (21) For then there will be great tribulation, such as has not been since the beginning of the world until this time, no, nor ever shall be. (22) And unless those days were shortened, no flesh would be saved; but for the elect's sake those days will be shortened."

(23) "Then if anyone says to you, 'Look, here is the Christ!' or 'There!' do not believe it. (24) For false christs and false prophets will rise and show great signs and wonders to deceive, if possible, even the elect. (25) See, I have told you beforehand."

(26) "Therefore if they say to you, 'Look, He is in the desert!' do not go out; or 'Look, He is in the inner rooms!' do not believe it."

The abomination of desolation marks the middle of Daniel's final week, a definitive marking of time concerning Daniel's people Israel

(Dan. 9:24-27). This passage from Daniel has all the salient features that distinguish prophetic writings.

The Character of Prophecy

1. It is specifically about Daniel's people (Dan. 9:24). The subject of prophecy is Israel.

2. It is about the marking of time concerning Israel on the earth (Dan. 9:24).

3. It is about God's government of the earth. In this case, it is counting the time involved with the three remaining Gentile world dynasties that rule over and afflict Daniel's people (Dan. 9:24-27). The exception is Babylon, which had already passed by the time of this prophecy.

In the passage above from Matthew 24, Jesus is speaking about Jewish time and Jewish signs. It is obvious He is not speaking of the church or to the church. If Daniel's revelations were about his people and Jesus is referring to Daniel's prophecies, then Jesus is also speaking prophetically to Israel. The whole nature of the passage bears this out. Further, He is directly speaking to a Jewish remnant in the midst of Israel in the end. This Jewish remnant is the elect He often refers to – in this case the remnant cannot be deceived by false christs and false prophets.[45] Why? Because God sealed them and keeps them as the elect, chosen by Him (Mark 13:20). But the rest of the nation will be greatly deceived in the end by false christs and false prophets showing great signs and wonders to deceive. It is their nature and it is the character of their religion – "The Jew seeks after a sign..."

He who comes in his own name

Even more condemning in the end is how the nation of Israel will receive the antichrist. He will be the one who comes in his own name, that they will receive in direct contrast to Jesus Christ having come in His Father's name (John 5:43).[46] The antichrist will do this:

Revelation 13:13-14

"He performs great signs, so that he even makes fire come down from heaven on the earth in the sight of men. And he deceives those who dwell on the earth by those signs which he was granted to do in the sight of the beast, telling those who dwell on the earth to make an image to the beast who was wounded by the sword and lived."

The calling down fire from heaven is a noteworthy sign to the nation of Israel. For the purpose of deceiving Israel, the antichrist will mimic the prophet Elijah. It was the test and proof to Israel that Jehovah is the one true God (I Kings 18:19-40). In the end Israel will go after the antichrist, which is the working of Satan, with all power, signs, and lying wonders.

Worldly wisdom of the Gentiles

If we speak of the Greeks 'seeking after wisdom,' we are speaking in general of the other part of the unbelieving world. They would shun ecclesiastical pretentions and religious superstition. Through the wisdom of the world they seek to reason and prove that God does not exist. By their science, contemporary liberal philosophies, and higher reasoning they strive to become independent of God and simply apostate. Faith in God is a superstition to them, the cross of Christ nothing but foolishness. Their faith is in the sciences and philosophies for the explanation of all the mysteries of life and the universe. Human intellect and human accomplishment are exalted, and by it man is exalted to the exclusion of God, and even to the position of God.

Romans 1:19-22

"...because what may be known of God is manifest in them, for God has shown it to them. (20) For since the creation of the world His invisible attributes are clearly seen, being understood by the things that are made, even His eternal power and Godhead, so that they are without excuse, (21) because, although they

knew God, they did not glorify Him as God, nor were thankful, but became futile in their thoughts, and their foolish hearts were darkened. (22) Professing to be wise, they became fools,"

The world through wisdom did not know God. Presently through their scientific exploration and liberal thinking they create a bias against God. It has become this way for much of the Gentile world. Has God not made foolish the wisdom of this world? In the end the instruments of worldly evil will take on a form of full and open rebellion and apostasy against God. This is because the dragon will be kicked out of the heavens down to the earth and he will know his time is short (Rev. 12:9, 12). He gives all his power to the two beasts, and to the first, his throne and authority (Rev. 13:1-2, 7, 12). In order for the 4th beast of Daniel to rise up out of the bottomless pit (Rev. 17:8), it will have to throw off and destroy all the religious influence and superstitions of the Mystery, Babylon the Great, the harlot that has rode its back for centuries (Rev. 17:3-6, 16-17).

1 Corinthians 1:24-31

"...but to those who are called, both Jews and Greeks, Christ the power of God and the wisdom of God. (25) Because the foolishness of God is wiser than men, and the weakness of God is stronger than men.

(26) For you see your calling, brethren, that not many wise according to the flesh, not many mighty, not many noble, are called. (27) But God has chosen the foolish things of the world to put to shame the wise, and God has chosen the weak things of the world to put to shame the things which are mighty; (28) and the base things of the world and the things which are despised God has chosen, and the things which are not, to bring to nothing the things that are, (29) that no flesh should glory in His presence. (30) But of Him you are in Christ Jesus, who became for us wisdom from God—and righteousness and sanctification and redemption— (31) that, as it is written, "He who glories, let him glory in the Lord."

The Wisdom of the World is only foolishness to God

For the believer, Christ is the power and wisdom of God. The Spirit then goes on to show how the wise and the mighty of this world are brought to naught by the calling and choice of God. In almost every verse the Spirit compares the wisdom and power of God with that of the world. Basically there is no comparison. The weakness of God is stronger than the mightiest of men, the foolishness of God wiser than the wisest of men. And this is what the believer is in Christ Jesus and what Christ has been made for us. And once again, it being God's choice and God's calling, and being God's work alone, there will never be any flesh boasting in His presence.

"But of Him you are in Christ Jesus, who became for us wisdom from God."

1 Corinthians 2:6-7

"However, we speak wisdom among those who are mature, yet not the wisdom of this age, nor of the rulers of this age, who are coming to nothing. But we speak the wisdom of God in a mystery, the hidden wisdom which God ordained before the ages for our glory,"

Christ has become for us the wisdom of God. In Him and through Him we have the mind of Christ. By His Spirit given to us we know the deep things of God. And this wisdom that Christ has become for us will always trump the wisdom of this world (I Cor. 2:10-16). He was ours and we were His before time began, so that the hidden wisdom of God that we are in Christ is not of the world.[47]

The manifold Wisdom of God is known through the Church

Ephesians 3:9-11

"...and to make all see what is the fellowship of the mystery, which from the beginning of the ages has been hidden in God who created all things through Jesus Christ; to the intent that now the manifold wisdom of God might be made known by the church to the

principalities and powers in the heavenly places, according to the eternal purpose which He accomplished in Christ Jesus our Lord,"

The multifaceted wisdom of God is made known by the church's existence. This was the eternal purpose of God in His counsels and plans. Such counsels existed in eternity past. Before time began we were found to be in Christ to the eternal glory of God and for the displaying of the gathered body of Christ in His glory (II Tim. 1:9). It will be throughout the ages to come that God will show the exceeding riches of His grace in His kindness toward us in Christ Jesus (Eph. 2:7). The church is the manifold wisdom of God displayed.

Ephesians 1:18-20

"...the eyes of your understanding being enlightened; that you may know what is the hope of His calling, what are the riches of the glory of His inheritance in the saints, and what is the exceeding greatness of His power toward us who believe, according to the working of His mighty power which He worked in Christ when He raised Him from the dead and seated Him at His right hand in the heavenly places,"

Philippians 3:21

"...who will transform our lowly body that it may be conformed to His glorious body, according to the working by which He is able even to subdue all things to Himself."

The resurrection of Christ – the resurrection of the Believer

The church will enter into this glory after our bodies are transformed and we are caught up from this earth. This event – the display of the exceeding greatness of God's power toward us – has already been demonstrated when God raised Christ from the dead (Eph. 1:18-23). According to the general content of I Cor. 15, the resurrection of Christ is intimately connected to the resurrection of the believer/ church. There He is called the firstfruits from among the dead. The body of Christ, the church, must be glorified in the same way as

He was glorified – His resurrection was the demonstration of it. His body must be joined to Him, not just by the Spirit presently in spiritual truth and understanding, but by physical presence through the display of God's exceedingly great power. He is the firstfruits from the dead, and the believer/church will be the many others.

Also in I Cor. 15 we clearly see a contrast between the first and second Adams – the first was of the earth, made of dust. The second man, the Son of Man, is from heaven. There remain those who are heavenly, destined to bear the image of the heavenly Man. We will be raised in glory, we will be raised in power (I Cor. 15:42-54). The first man was a living being, the last Adam a life-giving spirit. This should be clearly seen in two great realities of life in Christ. As the Son He gives life to whom He wills (John 5:21) and He is the resurrection life in the believer that eventually will swallow up mortality/corruption (I Cor. 15:51-55, II Cor. 5:1-5). According to God's counsels we will be transformed and conformed to Christ's image by the working of His power by which He is able to subdue all things.

We (believers) have the mind of Christ and have been given the Spirit of Truth. As Christ is the wisdom of God, so is made known by the existence of the church, His body, the manifold wisdom of God (Eph. 3:10). It will be our God's and our Father's good pleasure, in the ages to come, to display His wisdom and grace through the church seated in heavenly places in Christ Jesus (Eph. 2:6-7). So also, in the rapture of the church, when the Lord returns for us, will we be manifested in glory by the power of God in Christ. It will be according to the working of His mighty power, whereby He is able to subdue all things unto Himself. Then it will in fact be physically shown (for it is now only known by faith) that the church will be quickened by "the exceeding greatness of His power toward us who believe, according to the working of His mighty power which He worked in Christ when He raised Him from the dead and seated Him at His right hand in the heavenly places..." (Eph. 1:17-23)

Once again, this is God's sovereign work according to His eternal counsels and purpose, and for His eternal glory in Christ. This is what God has made Jesus Christ to be for us. He is both the resurrection and the life. Truly then, Christ has been made to those who are called, both the power of God and the wisdom of God.

Chapter 14: Endnotes

[44] Many of the doctrinal systems of theology struggle with the question, 'What to do with Israel, the descendants of Abraham after the flesh?' Here I will address those systems that have Israel replaced by the church and basically see the nation of Israel ceasing to exist, at least the nation no longer existing according to the flesh. These particular systems may view the nation of Israel as always having been the church, even when they were delivered out of Egypt and pass through the Red Sea. So in some cases the concept is not simply the church replacing Israel at some point in time, but that Israel was always the church and the church is always the real nation of Israel. As you can see this can get very confusing when trying to keep straight the what, when, where, and how concerning this substitution or elimination or spiritualization that these systems are proposing.

I believe the Scriptures and the mind of God show this: Israel is a real nation. They are the physical descendants of Abraham after the flesh – physical fleshly descent by natural birth. They are a people and a nation in the flesh. Their religion is of the flesh and of the senses – it is truly a walk by the flesh and senses. The law is not of faith (Gal. 3:11-12), so Judaism cannot be a walk by faith (II Cor. 5:7). By their religion and birth they are always connected to the flesh. God's separation of Israel was from the Gentiles in the world, but it was never a separation apart from the world itself. Israel always remains a part of the world and connected to the world. God's calling of Israel is an earthly calling. By it they are a people after the flesh connected to this earth and the Promised Land.

God made promises to this nation, the physical descendants of Abraham. These promises were made unconditionally. The main point I make is that God made promises to the physical line of descendants of Abraham and He will never change or rescind those promises, but will remain absolutely faithful to fulfill His promises to them. How can God do otherwise? We see many of these promises made in Genesis, but other promises to David and his linage. If God makes any promise, He must be faithful in time to fulfill that exact promise – this is the faithfulness of God as a divine attribute. Unconditional promises from God are fulfilled by Him through sovereign choice and sovereign grace. Teaching point: every choice God makes is sovereign and all grace from God is sovereign – this defines the choice of God and the grace of God and eliminates any Arminian thought from the equation.

We often fail to understand the dynamics of the covenant of promise given to Abraham and confirmed in his One Seed, who is Christ (Gal. 3, 4). The promises are unconditional and are all deposited in Jesus Christ (II Cor. 1:18-20). The responsibility of man or Abraham has no involvement with this covenant. This covenant is not an agreement between two parties as we commonly think of covenant. It was an agreement of one party, of God with Himself alone. No mediator for this covenant, because there weren't two parties or two conditions to be met on two different sides (Gal. 3:19-20). Again, it was simply unconditional promises requiring God to remain faithful for their fulfillment – this is sovereign grace.

The point I try to show is that the nation of Israel exists today as they did back in the wilderness in front of Mt. Sinai, and that these people of physical descent from Abraham are still part of the plan and counsel of God. I show Israel as distinct from the body of Christ, the church. Now there would be numerous ways to approach this task, but we'll look at what Jesus says in Luke 13:34-35 and Matt. 23:37-39.

Luke 13:34-35

"O Jerusalem, Jerusalem, the one who kills the prophets and stones those who are sent to her! How often I wanted to gather your children together, as a hen gathers her brood under her wings, but you were not willing! See! Your house is left to you desolate; and assuredly, I say to you, you shall not see Me until the time comes when you say, 'Blessed is He who comes in the name of the Lord!' "

He speaks to the city, but the city didn't kill the prophets God sent. Rather the people and the leaders representing the nation were responsible. They were guilty of all the blood of their prophets (Matt. 23:29-36). Jesus is speaking to the nation of Israel, the descendants of Abraham according to the flesh. He is not speaking to the body of Christ! When He says your house is left to you desolate He is again speaking directly to Israel. The church is not left desolate for nearly two thousand years! He says, "... assuredly, I say to you, you shall not see Me until the time comes..." Who is He speaking to? Is it to the church or Israel? Obviously He is speaking to Israel. They saw Him at that time, but the house of Israel would become desolate for a long time, as set aside by God. (Jesus saying, "Your house..." is referring to one of two things or both: the Jews as the house of God and/or the temple that was the center of the worship and practice of Judaism. Regardless it is related to Israel, not the church, the body of Christ)

It is a good thing that the gifts and callings of God are without repentance. Jesus tells Israel they would not see Him again until... How will this be fulfilled? Jesus Christ, the Messiah of Israel, will appear a second time to this nation. How will this be different? In the end God will prepare a Jewish remnant of His choice (elect) and will pour out His Spirit on them, before the great and terrible day of the Lord. It will be these who will be crying out for deliverance and vengeance during Jacob's trouble (Luke 18:1-8). These will be His elect who will say when He appears again to the nation, "Blessed is He who comes in the name of Jehovah!"

It should be obvious that Jesus is speaking to the nation of Israel and not the church. It should be obvious that it is the nation of Israel made desolate and not the church. The two passages span a long period of time where this nation will not see Him, having seen Him at the time of His speaking. This house of Israel remains desolate for nearly two thousand years. When Jesus says, 'I will build my church', is this in desolation? The gates of hell will not prevail against it? Does this sound like a desolate house? Further, He promises He will appear again, at some future point in time, to this house made desolate. His elect remnant, chosen by God out of unbelieving Israel, animated by the Spirit poured out on them before His appearing again to them, cannot be deceived by a false messiah (Matt. 24:22-24). Jesus is the true Messiah to Israel, who comes to the nation as the anointed Servant of Jehovah – "...until you say, 'Blessed is He who comes in the name of the Lord!'"

In the first book of this series I made the point that Messiah comes to Israel two different times. This is exactly what Jesus is speaking of in these passages. His first coming to Israel was based on the responsibility of Israel, it being the final testing of the principle of responsibility in man by God. The testing of man in responsibility always proves his failure. Israel rejected their Messiah, their King. The second coming of Messiah to Israel is by sovereign power, choice, and grace. These are the opposite principles from that of responsibility in man. The first coming to Israel was doomed to failure, and for the nation it was a complete failure. The second coming cannot fail for it is the sovereign work of God, and has no dependence on the responsibility of Israel.

[45] Jesus refers to the end-time Jewish remnant as the elect in a number of places: Matt. 24:22, 24, and 31; Mark 13:20, 22, and 27; and Luke 18:7. These all occur during prophetic statements He makes. Also during these prophetic statements He is often speaking directly to the remnant – "... when you see the abomination of desolation," is a sign and direct warning

to them to flee Judea for the mountains. It is the end-time Jewish remnant who will see all these signs and warnings. It is the remnant that should hope their flight is not in the winter or on the Sabbath. The Old Testament prophecies do refer to a Jewish remnant in the end (Is. 1:9, 8:17-18, 10:20-23, 11:11, 16, 28:5, 65:9, 22, Jer. 23:3, 31:1-14, Joel 2:32, Micah 2:12, 4:7, 5:3, 7-8, 7:18, Zeph. 3:8-15, Zech. 8:7-13, Rom. 9:27). These are the elect Jesus speaks of prophetically as the great Prophet to Israel to whom Moses referred.

Jesus saying, "when you see the abomination of desolation," He is speaking of the event that begins the conclusion of the last three and a half years of Gentile world power – the time of Jacob's trouble (Jer. 30:7). This does not refer to Titus of the Romans in 70 AD. We know this to be true when we look at the verses that follow His statement:

Matthew 24:21-22

"For then there will be great tribulation, such as has not been since the beginning of the world until this time, no, nor ever shall be. And unless those days were shortened, no flesh would be saved; but for the elect's sake those days will be shortened."

Two things to note: the abomination of desolation brings on the great tribulation – the most horrific time ever seen or experienced on the face of the earth. That did not happen in 70 AD with the destruction of Jerusalem and the temple. Also Jesus says that the days of the great tribulation were shortened for the elect's sake (the Jewish remnant) – this means shortened to three and a half years. It does not refer to nearly two thousand years of time.

With the understanding from the prophetic scriptures that there, in fact, will be a Jewish remnant awaiting a Messianic Deliverer (Rev. 7:1-8), a remnant on which the Spirit of God will be poured out upon before the great and terrible Day of the Lord (Joel 2:28-32), then we are better assured that it is not the church waiting for His appearing. Rather, it will be a Jewish remnant waiting according to prophecy, with Jewish hopes of deliverance from oppressive Gentile powers, and restoration in their Promised Land. For it to be the church waiting with the remnant on the earth for the Day of the Lord, or the church seen and believed to be this elect group enduring the most horrific time the world has ever known, is simply a violation of the proper understanding of prophetic biblical principles. Also, as I have mentioned previously, God does not deal with two separate and distinct callings at the same time.

[46] The testimony given in John 5 concerning Jesus Christ as sent by God to Israel is threefold. It is a testimony rendered against Israel. First, John the Baptist testified the truth concerning who Jesus was, and Israel had heard this testimony (John 5:33-35). Second, and a much greater testimony, are the powerful works that He did. These were given to Him by the Father to accomplish and they are a witness that He was sent by the Father (John 5:36). Third, the Father Himself has testified concerning who Jesus was, speaking from the heavens above (John 5:37). There is one more testimony that Israel would not receive because they did not have God's word abiding in them – it is how the Scriptures testify of Christ (John 5:38-40). Eternal life is found in the Father and the Son (John 5:26). The Jews mistakenly thought this was found in the Scriptures or their law. They were on the wrong side of every testimony of truth presented here.

[47] All things revealed in Scripture as spiritual truths and realities in God's counsels before the foundations of the world are all the things set apart from the world. They are the things that have no relationship with the created world or earth (this is a great Scriptural principle in understanding). The believer/church is found in Christ before time begins and before the world (Eph. 1:4, II Tim. 1:9, and Titus 1:2). Our calling is heavenly, and not of the earth or world (Heb. 3:1). Jesus said, "They are not of the world, just as I am not of the world." (John 17:14, 16, 15:19) The mystery given to Paul to reveal, which was not revealed until Christ was glorified and the Spirit sent down, was hidden in God before time began and before the foundations of the world. All aspects of this mystery were hidden in God and separate from the world. The wisdom of God in Christ towards the believer/church is all part of this mystery – that is why the Spirit says through Paul, "But we speak the wisdom of God in a mystery, *the hidden wisdom which God ordained before the ages for our glory.*"

Notes

Chapter 15:

The Resurrection and the Life

ne of the most notable bible passages is referred to in the title of this chapter. It is one Christians often like to find in the Scriptures and read. The words themselves are somehow comforting to the believer, giving a peace that is simply beyond understanding. We love to picture Jesus making this declaration and wish for one moment we were standing by Martha to hear His words.

John 11:25

"Jesus said to her, "I am the resurrection and the life."

If we read the entire chapter we know that this was a stressful situation. There were all kinds of questions swarming around the circumstances. Where was Jesus when Lazarus was so desperately sick? Why did He delay coming to help? If He would have been there in Bethany this never would have happened. He had healed so many! Now death had come in and all was lost. It was now a hopeless and irreversible situation. These words of His to Martha were meant to comfort her in her grief.

As is usually the case, we will find that the Lord's words go well beyond the immediate stressful situation He is in. They go much further than words of comfort to the grieving. They even go well beyond the physical resurrection of His close friend Lazarus that was soon to take place. And this is where we must go as believers – to know and fully comprehend His words spoken here, even if it was hidden from this struggling and grieving remnant gathered around the tomb.

The Father's Testimony

We can easily see in reading the chapter that all the circumstances were engineered and controlled by Jesus. The sickness, the delay in responding, the questions, the four days in the tomb, and the testimony that corruption has now set in were all part of God's design.

John 11:4

"When Jesus heard that, He said, "This sickness is not unto death, but for the glory of God, that the Son of God may be glorified through it."

What would be accomplished was a grand testimony of Jesus Christ being the Son of God, and He being displayed and glorified through this event. The raising of Lazarus from the dead was the Father's testimony to all who could see that Jesus was His Son, sent into the world by Him (John 11:41-43). This would be the understanding of the circumstances we find in the chapter, and how it glorified God. However, as previously mentioned, His words reach far beyond these circumstances, and speak of truths that far outweigh the raising of Lazarus.

Jesus Christ is our Life

Jesus Christ is the resurrection and the life. He is this for all believers. As for our life, He is it. He is our life (Gal. 2:20, Col. 3:3-4). We possess eternal life, because we have the Son.

1 John 5:11-12

"And this is the testimony: that God has given us eternal life, and this life is in His Son. He who has the Son has life; he who does not have the Son of God does not have life."

Jesus saying, 'I am the life' goes even beyond the eternal life in every believer. The raising of Lazarus was a wonderful demonstration of God's power and glory, and only God could have accomplished this. We, as believers, given eternal life by the Son (John 17:2-3) are another example of something only God can accomplish (John 5:21-26). We have the Son and therefore possess eternal life. This life however, is the foundational truth upon which all our Christian hopes and desires exist. This life is Christ in us, and Christ in us is the believer's hope of glory (Col. 1:26-27).

2 Corinthians 5:4-5

"For we who are in this tent groan, being burdened, not because we want to be unclothed, but further clothed, that mortality may be swallowed up by life. Now He who has prepared us for this very thing is God, who also has given us the Spirit as a guarantee."

The Life that swallows up Mortality

It is Christ in us, the eternal life we now possess, that will be the power in our bodies that will swallow up our mortality in the rapture of the church. It is the life of Christ by which mortality puts on immortality. And we see that God has prepared us for this very thing. God glorifying our bodies by conforming them to the image of His Son has been His counsel from before the foundations of the world (Rom. 8:29-30). His Spirit given to us is the guarantee that all will be accomplished according to His plan.

Romans 8:11

"But if the Spirit of Him who raised Jesus from the dead dwells in you, He who raised Christ from the dead will also give life to your mortal bodies through His Spirit who dwells in you."

By His Spirit, the life we have will overwhelm the mortality of our flesh through the sovereign work and power of God. We will be changed (I Cor. 15:51). We will be glorified (Rom. 8:30). For the believer, Jesus Christ has abolished death, and brought life and immortality to light through the gospel (II Tim. 1:10).

The Resurrection that swallows up Corruption

Jesus also is the 'resurrection.' He was this for Lazarus by the power of God, but only in a temporary way. Lazarus eventually died again. Jesus truly is the resurrection for all believers who have fallen asleep in Christ. Jesus raised up from among the dead has become the firstfruits of those who have fallen asleep (I Cor. 15:20).

1 Corinthians 15:23

"But each one in his own order: Christ the firstfruits, afterward those who are Christ's at His coming."

At the coming of Christ for the church, the dead in Christ will rise first. That which has been corrupted will put on incorruption. In a moment, in the twinkling of an eye, the dead in Christ will be raised incorruptible (I Cor. 15:52). It will be according to these words:

1 Corinthians 15:42-45

"So also is the resurrection of the dead. The body is sown in corruption, it is raised in incorruption. It is sown in dishonor, it is raised in glory. It is sown in weakness, it is raised in power. It is sown a natural body, it is raised a spiritual body. There is a natural body, and there is a spiritual body. And so it is written, "The first man Adam became a living being." The last Adam became a life-giving spirit."

Jesus Christ, the Son of Man, is a life-giving spirit to all those who are found in Christ, particularly for those who have fallen asleep in Him. Jesus is the resurrection and the life. At the rapture of the church, He is the resurrection for the dead in Christ, and the life for those who remain, changing mortality into immortality.

Paul's words detailing the Rapture – Christ, the Resurrection and the Life

1 Thessalonians 4:13-18

"But I do not want you to be ignorant, brethren, concerning those who have fallen asleep, lest you sorrow as others who have no hope. (14) For if we believe that Jesus died and rose again, even so God will bring with Him those who sleep in Jesus."

(15) "For this we say to you by the word of the Lord, that we who are alive and remain until the coming of the Lord will by no means precede those who are asleep. (16) For the Lord Himself will descend from heaven with a shout, with the voice of an archangel, and with the trumpet of God. And the dead in Christ will rise first. (17) Then we who are alive and remain shall be caught up together with them in the clouds to meet the Lord in the air. And thus we shall always be with the Lord. (18) Therefore comfort one another with these words."

These are the words of the Spirit through Paul concerning the specific details of the rapture event. We have discussed this passage in a previous chapter. It is the Lord's coming for the church, so that the body of Christ, from that point on will always be with the Lord. It is Christ as both the resurrection and the life of the church. It is Jesus saying to Martha: (John 11:25-26)

"I am the resurrection and the life. He who believes in Me, though he may die, he shall live. And whoever lives and believes in Me shall never die. Do you believe this?"

Christ's words detailing the Rapture – Christ, the Resurrection and the Life

- *"He who believes in Me, though he may die, he shall live."* This is the exact same intention of the Spirit of God, when speaking through Paul in describing the rapture of the church. Paul says, *"And the dead in Christ will rise first."* (I Thess. 4:16) That is those who believe in Him, those in Christ, even though they have died, He will raise them, and they will live. *"...though he may die, he shall live," is Resurrection.*

- *"And whoever lives and believes in Me shall never die."* This is the exact same intention of the Spirit of God speaking through Paul in Thessalonians as well, in the same passage about the rapture. Paul says, *"...we who are alive and remain until the coming of the Lord will by no means precede those who are asleep... then we who are alive and remain shall be caught up together with them in the clouds to meet the Lord in the air.* (I Thess. 4:15-17) That is those who believe in Christ, if they are alive when He comes, they continue living. These will be the ones who will never die. If the believer remains alive to the coming of the Lord for the church, he shall never die – this *is Life.*

Do you believe this? In John 14:1-4, Jesus speaks of the rapture in general terms. He is coming back for us to take us to where He went after He ascended. He was always excited about returning to His Father. Those He would eventually return for would have the same relationship with the Father as He. He desires for His brethren to be with Him there, with Him and the Father. But here in John 11:25-26, He gives a different aspect to the rapture event, one in which He Himself is the resurrection and the life. There is the intimate relationship and privilege side to this doctrine – these are His words in John 14. There is the other side of the doctrine which is the power and glory of God – these are His words in John 11. So He also says to Martha:

John 11:40

"Did I not say to you that if you would believe you would see the glory of God?"

By the rapture of the church we will enter into the glory of God. We will no longer be falling short (Rom. 3:23). This is the mystery: Christ in you, the hope of glory (Col. 1:26-27). It will be the realization of our hopes and Christian privilege. If you are a believer you will not only see the glory of God, but you will enter it, into the very presence of our Father. We will do this with Jesus Christ, for we have nothing and are nothing apart from Him. This is the blessed hope and constant expectation of the church.

Notes

Jesus Christ is the Resurrection and the Life. Without Him you will not have either. It is appointed unto man once to die and after that the judgment (Heb. 9:27). If it is judgment for you, it is because you don't have the Son, and you cannot possibly have life. It is Christ who is the believer's life. It is Christ as the believer's life that results in either resurrection or life swallowing up mortality. This is the believer's glorification. But if it is judgment for you, it is not glorification in Christ. It is judgment for you because you do not believe and you are not in Christ. You do not have the Son and so you do not have life – the life that results in resurrection and immortality. If it is judgment for you, this has its own fruits and results – condemnation and wrath.

Almost all mankind believes that there is something beyond death and the grave. Most are convinced of some sort of continuance and permanence of soul. In our reasoning we can place ourselves in this state, trusting and expecting for a favorable existence earned in some way by our present life. In this associated immortality of the soul we can exalt the 'self,' believing we have every right to a good outcome. This is easy for our minds to reason with, and we might say our reasoning is even justified.

God is the God who raises the dead. He is the God who is omnipotent. He is the God who will take a physical body that has been dead and corrupted in the grave for thousands of years, and raise it up. He is the God who does this. He is the God who raises the dead out of the dust. This is what is mind boggling for the unbeliever. You can reason some sort of immortality to the soul that will stretch beyond death. But this you can't imagine. This is silly and foolishness. This is fantasy. A physical body corrupted and returned to dust, God will put back together again. Not only raised back to living, but immortalized and glorified.

Here is the catch. We say this is foolishness and fantasy, because we know this is something that man cannot accomplish. The raising of the dead takes man, and his efforts and reasoning, out of the equation. The raising of the dead is something only an omnipotent God can do. The believer's faith is in the God who raises the dead. The believer believes in the God who raised Christ up from among the dead. And Christ has become for us the Resurrection and the Life.

1 John 5:10-12

"He who believes in the Son of God has the witness in himself; he who does not believe God has made Him a liar, because he has not believed the testimony that God has given of His Son. (11) And this is the testimony: that God has given us eternal life, and this life is in His Son. (12) He who has the Son has life; he who does not have the Son of God does not have life."

If you are an unbeliever and have read this entire book, then God has quickened your conscience and is using His Word in this writing to draw you to Christ. He has chosen you and called you, and draws you to faith in Christ, in His death and shed blood. This is the only way you can have the Son. It is the only way you can have life. When you have the Son, He will be for you, the Resurrection and the Life.

But if you refuse the Son you do not have Him as life and you make God out to be a liar. How is this? God has sent the Son and testified as to exactly who He is – the very Son of God in human flesh. Without Him, the life you have on your own is from Adam. If you love your life here, all will be lost. God has already judged and condemned that life when He chased Adam out of the garden. God has proven the Adam life to be utterly depraved. When Christ was rejected as Messiah it sealed the coming judgment and condemnation of the entire world.

If you like the world it is because you belong to it as part of it. You are comfortable with your world and your life. You will not want Him to return, because when He does return, He will change the world by judgment. You do not want Him changing your world and judging your life. You do not want Him here at all. But He is the One who has bought the world. It is part of His inheritance and He returns to exercise His power over it and make it right. When He returns you will be found with the world, and with all those who will be mourning at the sight of Him.

Revelation 1:7

"Behold, He is coming with clouds, and every eye will see Him, even they who pierced Him. And all the tribes of the earth will mourn because of Him."

I know that you are thinking that you will be alright, but without the Son all is lost. At His return to this world the outcome will not be good for you.

Malachi 3:2

"But who can endure the day of His coming?
And who can stand when He appears?"

Can you stand before Him on that day? Will you have confidence before Him at His appearing? Will you say this is the One whom I love and have been longing for? Turn now to the blood of Jesus Christ and faith in that blood; it is your only hope of salvation. Perhaps God is calling you...

Then you will have the Son, and you will have life. Then the affections of your heart will grow for Him. You will know that He has left you this promise, "I will come again, and receive you unto myself, that where I am, there ye may be also." And you will respond with the rest of us, "Amen, Even so, come, Lord Jesus."